COMANCHE DAYS

BICENTENNIAL SERIES IN AMERICAN STUDIES

III

ALBERT S. GILLES, SR. studied law in Oklahoma and was admitted to the bar of that state in 1913. Now retired after many years spent in the practice of law, he lives in Norman and pursues the second career of writing on which he embarked in his seventies. His articles on Indian and frontier subjects have appeared in a number of magazines.

COMANCHE

DAYS

ALBERT S. GILLES, SR.

SMU PRESS • DALLAS

© 1974 • Southern Methodist University Press • Dallas
Library of Congress Catalog Card Number: 74-77543
ISBN: 0-87074-139-X

The publication of this volume

was made possible

through the generosity of

MRS. EUGENE MC DERMOTT and THE MC DERMOTT FOUNDATION

and

PAUL F. BOLLER, JR.

To
the memory of
THE OLD FELLOWS, COMANCHE WARRIORS
who gave me their friendship
and to
the memory of
BENETTA BRUDNO
who over ten years spent in
helping me prepare this book—
memory dredging, researching, writing,
rewriting—never wavered in her
faith in the merits of the material
here presented

CONTENTS

PREFACE

DEAR BENETTA:

You sent me a clipping with the picture of a gravestone. The clipping is from a Dallas paper; its dateline is Comanche Gap, and it is written by one of the paper's columnists. The markings on the gravestone read, "John and Jane Riggs Murdered by Comanche Indians Mar 16, 1859." You penciled a question on the margin of the clipping, "Why should I like people who did this?"

I wonder if I can tell you. You ask me because my people took me into the Comanche country when the present century was starting its second year. They started a trading store and the Comanches became their customers. In picking a location for his trading store, Dad chose a little inland town, Faxon, Oklahoma Territory. It was twenty miles from Lawton, county seat of Comanche County and our nearest railhead. This Faxon no longer exists. It has been a wheat farm for many years. There were a large number of Comanche families living on their allotments—up and down West Cache, Blue Beaver, and Post Oak Creeks.

Dad and Mother came first to the Kansas frontier, he from Vermont, via some years in the Union Army during the Civil War, she from Kentucky, where she saw both armies march. She hid out a number of nights, with her mother and the other children, when the

Bushwhackers were near. Their hopes were that the raiders would be satisfied with driving away their stock and burning the house and other buildings, without hunting up the family and destroying them as well. Because of a crippled leg, her father wasn't accepted by the Union army; but he was away, serving in the home guard.

It was so simple for us. We never had an Indian problem. Having no traditions, for or against, when an Indian came into the store, we extended to him the same courteous treatment we rendered a white customer. The courtesy was returned by the Indian.

I wasn't aware there was an Indian problem. Then I realized there were people around us who were violently anti-Indian. It's normal for the average person to insist on fair play, and I found myself coming to the Indian's defense. I was in my fifteenth year, had my growth, and I suppose felt I had man status.

Now as I analyze those troubled white people, from the distance of years, I realize they were definitely lower middle class. Dad first cataloged them for me. I worried to him about a certain family's attitude. I had developed a certain friendliness toward the family. Then one day the man made a remark which sounded so narrow-minded it left me with an uncomfortable feeling. Dad gave me a typical Yankee answer. "You will have to realize, son," he said, "So-and-so is small potatoes, and few to the hill."

All readers of American history know Indians committed atrocities. But because the Comanche claimed, and tried to defend, thousands of square miles of territory with hundreds of miles of boundary, he came in contact with many more people, white and Indian, than any other tribe in the United States. His written history began in about 1704, and from then until his final surrender at Fort Sill in 1875 he fought a 171 years' continuous war. Only his enemy changed, from time to time.

But here is something that needs to be kept in mind. Many atrocities were committed by vicious white men disguised as Indians. Their acts too were charged up to the Indians, just as your clipping states; later three white men were hanged for the murders of Mr. and Mrs. Riggs. It shouldn't be out of order to suggest that though this took place 107 years ago, *the markings on the gravestone have never been corrected.*

But back to Comanche land, and the years I lived around these Indians. I'm sure many of the complaining homesteaders were living on their own land for the first time in their lives, and it is entirely possible the generation preceding them were tenant farmers also. Many of them complained bitterly because the Comanche was allowed to choose his allotment and the homesteaders drew for the remainder. The Comanche was smart enough to allot land along the streams, securing for himself and his progeny valley and bottomland, as well as timber and water.

Even at fifteen, my Scottish soul craved land so intensely I would have welcomed the poorest 160 acres in all Comanche County, as manna from heaven was welcomed by the Israelites. However, to the complaining homesteader the 160-acre farm for which he paid the government a $14.00 filing fee became a bitter taste in his mouth.

The Indian's land seemed superior to his—that was his thinking, at least. Today, the going price of the farms the homesteaders thought so inferior in 1902 is $20,000 and up. Many of them will bring a better price than the Indian's bottomland. They will produce a greater yield of wheat, one year with another.

But I tried to point out to the discontented that originally the Indian owned all this prairie paradise, stretching from horizon to horizon, excepting to the north. There a line of blue haze marked the existence of the Wichita Mountains, calling to our attention the fact that the prairies weren't boundless after all. The government hadn't *given* the Indians anything. But the discontented pretended not to understand my reasoning. Besides, in spite of my size I was only a fifteen-year-old kid with a fifteen-year-old head, arguing with men.

Then, as now, a multitude of people professed not to consider the white man an invader, taking land from an established people, who were living the kind of life they wanted to live, when he took possession of the Americas. But to me, this was just as true when the white man took the bountiful timbered country east of the Cross Timbers away from the crop-growing Wichitas, and the great plains from the horse-buffalo culture people, as it was when he destroyed the Aztecs' Mexico City, burned their libraries, and carried off their gold.

Let us, you and I, narrow the matter down to the Comanche people and their troubles with the white man. It was a little over two hundred years after the European landed in America before the Comanche became aware of the white man's existence—that is, unless we take Emmor Harston's viewpoint and place the Comanche (he hadn't acquired the Comanche) name as the Indian with whom Captain Francisco Vásquez de Coronado dealt.

For the sake of lessening the field of argument, let's take the conventional viewpoint and say the Spanish at Sante Fe were the first white men to meet the Comanches (then called the Padoucas), around the year 1700. Soon the Comanches were to meet the French around Salina, Oklahoma.

Researchers into the past of the Comanche people have come up with three names they have called themselves—Hemenjh, Nerma, and Nimma. But each meant the same—The People. And in my time, as well as in 1934, when Wallace and Hoebel were doing research for their book, *The Comanches: Lords of the South Plains,* if you asked one of the "Old Fellows": "What does Comanche mean?" he would reply, "The People." It seems to have been the Crows who gave them the name Padoucas. Later the Utes gave them the name that through various spellings became Comanche.

Long before they knew there was such a thing as a white man, they began putting together their inland empire, *Comancheria.* They built their empire as legitimately, by much the same method, and at approximately the same time as Charlemagne did his in Europe. They thoroughly whipped one enemy at a time until they consolidated the land they desired to hold. One by one, they joyously fought and completely whipped the Utes, Pawnees, Osages, Tonkawas, Apaches, Navahos, and numerous small tribes.

It is a bit hard to define Comancheria's northern boundary. At one time or another the Comanches controlled the great plains from the Missouri River in North Dakota south to the Rio Grande. Much of Old Mexico became raiding territory for them. On at least one occasion they raided as far south as Durango, 1500 miles, and they marketed their surplus horses to tribes living in Canada.

They allowed nature to prescribe their eastern boundary. Their love for the great sweeping prairies caused them, like the buffalo, to turn back when they came to the timber. The term Cross Timbers came to mean "Where the trees began," and it became Comancheria's eastern boundary, from approximately Wichita, Kansas, to the Neches River in East Texas.

Roughly, the Rockies became their western boundary. One group wandered westward, however, and made their home in Southern California. Numerous Comanche groups wintered in the canyons along the Rockies' eastern slopes. They did raid across New Mexico and Arizona. In time they seem to have drawn their empire's boundary to conform with the grazing habits of the southern herd of buffalo, and thus they established their guardianship over that multitude of beasts. Some writers contend they even herded the buffalo, to the extent of turning bunches of the huge animals back to the east, when they found them grazing too far westward from the main herd.

The northern group guarding the empire must have influenced history. They stopped the northward and eastward advance of the Spanish and the southward and westward advance of the French. Please remember, this was long before the Louisiana Purchase and the uniting of the Republic of Texas with the Union. One can easily imagine armed conflict between forces of these two powers over the possession of this huge territory.

Finally the Comanche seems to have settled on the Arkansas River valley as his northern boundary. More and more, he grew to like the milder climate he found, as he shifted his activities southward. It was a contrast to the *idaho* (cold) of the country to the north and northwest. Later, he allowed the Kiowa to take over the Arkansas valley. These newcomers were being driven south from their Dakota holdings by a westward movement of Indians with firearms from Minnesota and Wisconsin. Then, making peace with the Cheyennes and Arapahos, he allowed them to take over territory in Kansas north of the Kiowas. With these three buffer tribes protecting him from the north, he had more men and time to defend and extend his Oklahoma and Texas holdings.

The Mexican government gave the Comanches little trouble in Texas. Records indicate that when the Comanches visited San Antonio, the principal town in Texas, the Mexican town fathers not only provided guards for the Indians' horses, but furnished the number of beeves the visitors requisitioned.

Comanche braves participated in riding, roping, and racing events —forerunner of today's rodeos, staged by the Mexicans. Because of his success in competing with the best of the Mexican talent, Chief Horseback, the last war chief of the Comanches, was given the name Tut-huh-yet Nau-qua-hip. This translates as "Big War Chief Champion Rider."

In Texas, the constant inching westward of white settlers caused the Comanches concern, and they reacted violently. In reading early

Texas history you often find, in substance, this expression: "The Comanches delayed the settlement of Texas by at least fifty years."

Their Oklahoma troubles came from a different source. The part of Oklahoma lying east of Cross Timbers was occupied by the Wichitas and their friends, while the prairie to the west of this line was part of Comanchería.

You are from the well-settled East. It is hard for you to envision how perfectly the land on either side of the Cross Timber line was suited to the particular needs of the people who lived there for more years than we can even estimate. The Wichitas prized their land highly. It was rolling and hilly to mountainous, well watered, and covered with a wide variety of timber. To the west and north was a large variety of scrub oaks; in the valleys of the rivers and smaller streams grew the lofty water oak, gum, magnolia, and black walnut. In the marshy places, huge cypress trees were to be found in abundance, while the Ouachita Mountains in the southern area were covered with stately short-leaf pine.

The Wichitas valued especially the lower hills of southwestern Missouri, northwest Arkansas, and northeast Oklahoma. It was there they grew tobacco, their most valued crop. They planted and cultivated it extensively. It was their chief article for barter to the northern and western tribes. Their traditions say they found the tobacco plant growing as a weed in the southwest Missouri hills, and that all other Indians got their start of tobacco from them. These farmer-Indians lived in grass houses, grouped into small villages.

To the west of the Cross Timbers, with the exception of the range of the Wichita Mountains, lay a rolling to level prairie. It too was well watered, and it was covered with nourishing grasses—a perfect home for both the buffalo and its guardians, the Comanches. Here they had abundant, year-around graze for their vast herds of horses.

Among the traditions of old Comanche warriors, many had to do with the Wichitas. It was their contention that the two tribes, Wichita and Comanche, never made war one with the other. The Comanches depended upon the Wichitas to furnish them the gift of the Great Spirit, tobacco. In return, they traded horses and buffalo products.

Another tradition had to do with Cross Timbers as a boundary between the two tribes. According to Emmor Harston in *Comanche Land,* when Comanche horsemen came to the Cross Timbers they would say, "Si-ich-ka Tab-be Ka-esop" (The midday sun doesn't tell a lie), and turn back west. The Wichitas turned east.

But white settlers in the Old South, that is to say Dixie, found five tribes of settled agricultural Indians: Chickasaw, Choctaw, Creek, Seminole, and Cherokee. By the 1800s many of these Indians were operating well-stocked and prosperous plantations. They were owners of Negro slaves and were well-to-do—enough to cause the less prosperous whites to covet their holdings.

As it was to happen many times and to many other tribes, the United States government forced these settled and prosperous people to move, and white people were allowed to seize their holdings. In an involuntary exchange, they were given what is now Oklahoma. The army moved and settled them in the eastern part, east of the Cross Timbers. The western part was to be their hunting ground.

But the army, in its compulsory moving of these civilized Indians to what then was called Indian Territory, found its job far from completed. It had to remain and protect the tame Indians from the wild ones whose land they had preempted. The Wichitas were cut in two. Some were left in Missouri and Kansas; those living in Oklahoma were completely dispossessed. Those living in Texas were not disturbed, for the time being, as Texas was still Mexican territory.

The coming of the Civilized Indians made outlaws of the Comanches living in Oklahoma—though they were living on land they had occupied for uncounted years. If the Comanche withdrew, he would either have to move in with his Texas tribesmen or fight his way back north for land he had long since abandoned. Everything south of Red River and west of the 100th meridian was Mexican territory. There would be no one left from Red River north to protect his buffalo as they grazed their way northward in the spring and returned south in the fall.

A line of forts, from north to south, to the west of the civilized Indian settlements, was established by the army. Fort Towson was to guard against invasions of the Wichitas and Comanches from the south and southwest. Farther north and to the west was Fort Washita, and to the northeast, Fort Gibson.

Besides these permanent posts, a number of camps were set up to form an armed barrier between the newly established residents and the dispossessed. Only the outbreak of the Civil War in 1861 relieved the army of this guardianship. Most of the newly settled tribes allied themselves with the Confederacy. The Union troops from the forts were forced to withdraw to Kansas.

In 1834 the government organized the Dragoons, the army's first cavalry, to cope with the Comanches and other plains Indians. The four troops were assembled at Fort Gibson and placed under the command of General Leavenworth. They headed southwest through Oklahoma with the purpose of finding and, if possible, making a treaty with the Comanches.

The Dragoons, dressed in heavy wool clothes, were victims of the heat, bad water, and malaria. Their ranks thinned fast. Commander General Leavenworth was a casualty before the Dragoons found the Comanches. His successor in command crossed Red River to the west, into Mexican territory, before any Comanches were found. The artist George Catlin, who accompanied the expedition, left us a sketch of this first meeting.

The actions of government representatives, army and civilian, in the making of treaties with the Comanches and then failing to live up to their agreements can best be described as being on a par with the government's dealing with other Indians. Many of the treaty failures came about because Congress refused to provide the funds necessary to fulfill treaty obligations.

On the whole, we followed the pattern prescribed by Bismarck for the guidance of the German people. Like the Kaiser, we considered our treaties with the Comanches and other Indians as "just scraps of paper," as far as honoring the government's part of the agreements went. But the government never hesitated to use the army to secure compliance, down to the last letter, on the part of the Indians.

The treatment of the Indians of the Southwest by General Sam Houston, both as president of the Republic of Texas and later as governor of the State of Texas, is the bright spot in an otherwise shoddy array of American and Texan Indian dealings.

These governments had courts, the army, an organized Ranger force, and a multitude of other peace officers to enforce court edicts. In this connection, Sam Houston is quoted as saying, "I have never known of a treaty made with an Indian tribe that was *first violated by them*. But each is violated by the white man before the ink is dry."

The uneducated and unrepresented Indians stood alone. You probably recall the black mark on General Andrew Jackson's record. When referring to a decision handed down by Chief Justice Marshall upholding certain rights of the Indians, he said in effect, "The Court has made its decision. Now let's see them enforce it."

The longer a man lives and the more tasks he attempts, the more mistakes he makes, both in deed and in judgment. The man who does but little makes few mistakes, and he who does nothing makes none. My life has been long, my tasks many and varied—I have made many mistakes. Possibly I'm wrong in this; but as I view our government's and the Comanche's relations, from the meeting of the Dragoons and the Comanches in 1834 down to the day in 1875 when Quanah Parker led the remnant of the Quo-ha-die Te-jas—Antelope Eater band— into Fort Sill to their surrender, the Comanche had tried only to protect and preserve what he had fought for and considered his for upward of a thousand years.

Please remember: in 1834, our government was less than fifty years old, and Columbus's discovery was only 342 years in the past. But at the time the Comanches met up with the Spaniards at Sante Fe, in about 1704, anthropologists figure they had been a distinct tribe for at least a thousand years.

When mention is made of Indian atrocities, it is always with the inference that here is something no white man can even imagine committing, much less actually commit. But I ask you, have you read the printed records of the deeds committed by the bushwhacker- guerrilla bands of the Civil War period? These bands operated all the way from West Virginia into Kansas. You can find plenty of incidents, as bad as or worse than the Riggs episode, laid at the door of Quantrill and his band, operating throughout southern Missouri and eastern Kansas. His range was right next door to Oklahoma. In fact, his band was supposed to have retreated into Indian Territory from time to time to cool off when its own range became too hot.

Some day, when your stomach feels extra strong, read the story of Quantrill's raid on Lawrence, Kansas. Then decide if the wild Comanches were so inhuman after all, in comparison. The Lawrence outrage was committed by white men against the *white populace* of the *town*, not by the wildest stretch of imagination against a military objective. Banks and businesses were robbed and fired. Men, women, and children were robbed, made homeless, burned to death. Much of the town went up in flames.

The James boys, Jesse and Frank, and the three Younger brothers rode with Quantrill that day. Keep this in mind the next time you see these characters represented on the screen and TV as downtrodden, misunderstood, mother-loving boys at heart.

I hope all this may help you to answer your own question. Anyhow, you now have my way of thinking.

Sincerely,

ALBERT S. GILLES, SR.

COMANCHE DAYS

COMANCHE ANTIQUITY

IT WAS IN 1898 that I first studied about the Indian. That year Kansas adopted a new history textbook. The new book had a paragraph of five or six lines about the American Indian, the substance of which was that the Indian had been in America possibly two hundred to three hundred years before America was discovered by Columbus. As it was a new book, we may assume that this was the thinking of some of the leading historians.

Even when the so-called lost cities of central America were discovered, authorities here and abroad directly attributed European origins to them. Many theories have been advanced as to how the Indians' forefathers arrived in America and where they came from originally. Bering Strait and Siberia seem to have won out.

Some things are agreed upon. The Indians are of Mongolian extraction. They were originally barbarians, born of a stock which never, at any time, had been either civilized or associated with the influence of civilization. When the Indian came he was a man—Homo sapiens. No evidence has been found of the existence of preman in America.

There were and are, for the whole of Indian North America, six great linguistic superfamilies, each made up of numbers of separate stocks or families of speech. Each family usually consists of several languages which differ so much from one another that their common origin can be determined only by comparative lin-

3

guistics study; the superfamilies are even more varied than the large Indo-European stock or family with its Romance and Germanic and Slavic and Hindi divisions. [Theodora Krober, *Ishi in Two Worlds: A Biography of the Last Wild Indian in North America* (Berkeley: University of California Press, 1962), p. 15.]

In California alone there are 113 known dialects, some of them varying so greatly that to a person knowing one, another might be as unintelligible as German to a Frenchman. One can find estimates of 200 languages and 1,500 dialects for North America.

The Indian covered the two Americas like a blanket; he ranged from the Arctic to Tierra del Fuego, and did it on his two feet. Physically, Indians range from tall to short, from near black to near white. With the exception of the llama in Peru, the Indian was without a beast of burden until the Spanish brought the horse. When he first came he didn't even have a dog.

Europe had stone-age men, or near men, capable of making and using stone tools as early as 500,000 years ago; but if you had asked historians as late as our Civil War how long the Indian had been in America, the longest estimate probably would have been "about the time of Christ."

One evidence of the long period of time the Indian had been in America when the whites arrived is his development of Indian corn or maize. There is no such thing as wild corn. The Indian apparently developed it from a seed-bearing grass to a number of varieties of corn. He grew it in such diverse places as Maine with its short summers and northern Mexico with its near desert conditions. He grew it as an irrigated crop and a dry land planting. With but few exceptions, all tribes of the continental United States grew corn. Its development, of course, was by trial and error.

Not until a cowboy was hunting strayed cattle in 1926 near Folsom, New Mexico, was evidence found of an ancient stone culture. There, in association with Taylor's extinct bison bones, were found the Folsom spear and lance points. They differ from any other known point in having a flute, or groove, down the center of either side, as a bayonet is made, so that the wound can bleed.

Later the Sandia cave was found and excavated. Folsom flints were found at the top, but through various layers to the depth of eight feet were found much older flints—estimated to be twenty to twenty-five thousand years old.

Teilhard de Chardin, in his *Phenomenon of Man*, says: "It was in fact at the very dawn of the Neolithic age that man reached America."

He feels the movement of man to America was all part of the shifting when man finally emerged the complete Homo sapiens from the multitude of cousins, near man or preman, and divided up the earth among themselves—the white, yellow, brown, and black man, each taking his place, much as we find them today.

We know intelligent man was here in America during the days of the mastodon, hairy mammoth, tapir, and other prehistoric animals. We find his spear points with their bones. These animals ultimately perished through climatic changes, glacier periods, and cataclysms. Man lived through the fourth or Wisconsin ice age that left Pleistocene lakes, such as Bonneville, with an area of 20,000 square miles, in what is now a desert basin. Some geologists and anthropologists move his entrance back to 35,000, and a few to 38,000 years.

We know that the Indian was here before the volcanic period in the Sierra Nevadas, for his artifacts are found there under layers of lava. We know that he was here before one complete cave cycle occurred. We find his artifacts on a cave floor, encased in the mother-of-pearl-like substance that dripped from the cave roof. Now this is again a dry cave. Carleton S. Coon, in his *The Origin of Races*, estimates that this cycle covered a span of 25,000 years.

I have wondered why some anthropologist hasn't tried to date the Indian by the length of time it took him to cover the Americas afoot. He was carrying all his possessions, discovering his own trails, adapting himself to the climate, food supply, and terrain. What was his life expectancy? How far did the tide move each year? What caused him to move forward: curiosity, pressure from a following horde, depletion of food, or the search for a more favorable climate?

In tracing the antiquity of the Shoshone-Comanche tribes by language—glottochronology—one is constantly reminded of Rudolf Ludwig Karl Virchow's statement about languages: "When we know so little as we do yet, it behooves us to be modest in our theories." They are of the Uto-Aztecan language family, and the users of the languages are scattered from Canada into Old Mexico and west into California. After moving from the Oregon country the Shoshones seem to have taken root thousands of years ago in Idaho, northern Colorado, Wyoming, and Montana.

This is harsh country, with long cold winters and hot dry summers. The Shoshones were gatherers—that is to say, they were root-eaters and gathered nuts and grass seeds to supplement their game. Possibly because they had more people than the territory would support, many splinter tribes broke away from the parent tribe. I like to think of the Shoshones as the parent tribe.

Another way of tracing Shoshone origin is by the snake motif. As far as I am able to ascertain, all Shoshone splinter group Indians are also snake Indians and like the Comanches, use a snake sign. The Shoshone sign is the right forearm extended across the stomach, palm down, but held still. The Comanche sign starts the same way, then the arm is drawn backward and around the side of the body, with the forearm and hand undulating gently like a snake in motion. Because of this backward action, tribes coming in contact with the Comanche early called them "the Snakes going backward."

Lewis and Clark, possibly because they had Sacajawea with them as a guide, obtained considerable worthwhile information from the Shoshones. This included the story of a powerful people—relatives, who lived south on the Kansas River, who had once been part of the Shoshone people and from whom they obtained horses. The Shoshones told also of having followed the Missouri River out onto the prairies, but having been driven back by Indians armed with firearms. The invading Indians, in turn, had been driven from their homes farther east by the white man.

Primitive people living under the harsh temperature conditions faced by the Shoshone tend to become "today-people." That is to say, their energy is used up by reproduction and caring for their today's needs. They tend to forget yesterday and are too busy today to think of tomorrow. Passing of time registers but lightly. A tradition of something that happened hundreds or even thousands of years back suggests but a short passage of time to them.

Arminta Scott Spalding, a native of Mississippi, wrote an article for the Spring 1967 issue of the *Oklahoma Chronicle* dealing with the missionary work done among the Choctaws living along the Natchez Trace. She quotes an old Choctaw chief as follows: "The Choctaws are ignorant—they know when day comes and night comes. That's all they know. We expect to die in our old habits, but we want our children to do better." This was said in justifying Indian support of the missionary school.

Of the different stories I have heard as to why the Comanches left the parent tribe, one seems to tell the story properly and in few words.

"A long time ago the snake had two heads. For a long time the snake was hungry. Then one head went away, and the other head stayed at home."

To me, this tells the story of a people already separated in fact, but kindred and occupying the same general hunting ground. The separation was entirely friendly—one people glad to go, and the others glad to have them leave. This separation must have taken place before the coming of the horse, since the Shoshones related to Lewis and Clark how they had obtained their horses from their kinsmen who had gone south.

I am sure the Comanches did not leave for their new home all at one time. It would not have been logical. The country they were invading would not have supported so large a group, nor were they living in one group before they started out. It is more likely that they left one group at a time, as the country they were traversing would sustain them, first going east onto the prairie, then following the east side of the Rockies southward.

Emmor Harston had the opportunity to learn more Comanche tradition from the old chiefs and warriors, beginning when he went to Fort Sill as the son of an Indian licensed trader in 1871, than anyone living thirty years before him or thirty years after. In his *Comanche Land* he has the Comanche well down into Texas when Captain Francisco Vásquez Coronado mounted his expedition in 1540, hunting for the cities of gold. Harston has the Comanches guiding Coronado. One of the reasons he gives: all the names of places recorded by Coronado are Comanche names.

As a boy, Harston went to school with Comanche children, and having the knack of a linguist, he became fluent in the Comanche tongue. He went away to college and came back to live with them again. He became a special favorite of Horse Back and was on friendly terms with other old chiefs. His ability to speak the native tongue gave him a wonderful advantage. I am sure no one now living realizes better than I the opportunities afforded him to learn history from the Comanches' viewpoint. I followed him thirty years later and was also a trader's son. (Harston died before his book was compiled, and like Captain Pratt's *Battlefield and Classroom*, *Comanche Land* was assembled by other hands.)

I have always had a good deal of faith in the story of the snake having two heads and the inference that the separation was friendly.

Other incidents indicate the friendly attitude the Shoshones continued to maintain toward their "rich relatives." One winter in the late 1920s, I spent considerable time in Wyoming. One day at a depot, while I was waiting for a train, I noticed two nice-appearing young Indian men working on the street nearby. I went out and had a talk with them. They told me they were Shoshones, and seemed pleased when I told them I was from Oklahoma and had lived among the Comanches for a time. They were especially pleased that some of the Comanches had oil on their allotments. In a talk of possibly twenty minutes, I gathered the impression that to these two Shoshone boys at least, Comanche country was a bit of a faraway fairyland.

When we first meet the Comanche, accepting the 1700 date for the encounter, we find him in groups living in an L-shaped pattern. The top part of the L is north of the Arkansas River in Colorado, and according to Governor Juan Bautista de Anza of New Mexico they would have been the Yam-pa-ri-kas, or Root Eaters. And according to Harston they would have been the last Comanches to come from Shoshone land, probably from far to the west.

The upright part of the L extended south to the vicinity of Fort Stockton, Texas. The horizontal part of the L extended east to the Neches River. All along this L could be found groups or subtribes. Each group would have had a well-defined hunting territory; it was defending against all comers.

I now want to talk a bit about the tribes being already separated when the exodus began, and why I think they came to their new land in groups. Let us take their attitude toward one another and toward their other tribesmen. There never was an overall chief; there were only chiefs of bands. There never was an individual, or a governing body, that had the authority to call the tribe together. There is no indication that the tribe ever assembled as a whole.

Two or more groups were known to have joined forces to repel a strong enemy. But when the emergency was ended the groups went their separate ways.

Even the authority of the band chief was very limited. He could command no warrior to do any particular thing. Each warrior was his own man. He owned his own horses, his own fighting and hunting gear; and when he went on the war trail he was strictly a volunteer. At the start of an operation he carried his own food. If at any time during the trip he took a notion to go home, he was at liberty to leave.

But as long as he was a member of a war party he obeyed the leader's orders.

They had what they called war leaders, or raid leaders, men who had the reputation of leading successful raids against another tribe, or a white settlement, or in to Old Mexico to steal horses and women. They did not need to be chiefs, but they could be. If one decided to lead a raid, he sent a crier through the camp telling the objective of the raid and how many warriors were wanted. A leader was at liberty to refuse any volunteer, say for being too old or too young.

When the raiding group returned home, mission accomplished, the loot was divided. Many leaders refused to take more than a warrior's share, but some tried to fudge. Any leader who demanded too great a share became unpopular and often had trouble securing followers. I knew some old warriors who accused Comanche Chief Quanah Parker, when a young war leader, of claiming too much of the spoils.

The different bands appeared to have been loosely organized. Any time a warrior or a family group desired to leave and join another group they were free to do so, and no stigma was attached. If in the course of time they decided to return, they were free to do so. Not only were they at liberty to leave a group, but they were allowed to join any other group they wished—no permission was needed either to leave or to join a group.

This individual independence of action carried over into the camp life. Each individual, even the little folks, was responsible for his own behavior. In reading the observations of visitors, both civilian and military, to Comanche camps, one often finds the comment that there was no evidence of camp police such as had been observed among other tribes. Ridicule seems to have been the only governing force needed. Each individual desired the good opinion of the group as a whole. Nor was there such a thing as a Comanche working for another for hire. There were no hired girls, no hired baby sitters, no economic strata in Comanche society.

Though each writer seems to have had his own ideas concerning the total population of the Comanche tribe at high tide, they all agree that they were the best horse thieves and owned the greatest number of horses. They were great exponents of the horse-buffalo culture, and such a culture made multiple wives a necessity. Each individual warrior needed someone to care for his horses and his camp, and to tan

hides for the family's clothes. As a result of the Comanche's individual-
ism, polygamy became a social and economic necessity. There were
but two places for a Comanche woman—her father's camp and her
husband's camp. Concubinage and prostitution were not tolerated.

Harston names Tabbe Nanica, Ma-pe-cho-cuf-pe, Yellow Bear, and
Adeca Paph, along with Horse Back, as his principal authorities. Also,
he names A. L. Kroeber's Bulletin No. 78 of the Bureau of American
Ethnology as an authority for the movements and the probable time
of separation of the different "tribes who were of the Shoshonean
linguistic stock."

One of the ways philologists and anthropologists figure the length
of time one people has been separated from another, or from a parent
tribe, is by glottochronology, a comparison of languages. Taking fifty
or one hundred words common to both languages—such as father,
mother, deer, turkey—glottochronologists study the changes made in
the words. By a system of tables, developed over a long period of time,
they determine the number of years that have passed since the separation. They assume, of course, that the parent tribe's language has
changed the least.

By using this method, Alfred Louis Kroeber determined that the
Sososhone and Comanche tribes were separated approximately one
thousand years when they met the Spanish in 1700. If we go back to
the time all snake Indians spoke the same language, it would represent
a period of four thousand years. One writer suggests that "if we take
this same period in western European history, English, German and
Celtic would have been one language."

A check of the various names used by the Comanches and given
them by others may help to clear away some cobwebs. Let us take first
the word *Comanche*. The word has no root in either the Shoshone or
the Spanish tongue. It was assumed for many years to be of Spanish
origin. Then about 1942 Morris E. Opler solved the mystery.

The name comes from the Ute word *Komántcia*, meaning enemy.
Originally, it was applied to numerous tribes with whom the Utes
fought. But when the northern group of Comanches began giving the
Utes an especially hard time, driving them from their favorite winter
camping places (canyons opening back into the eastern side of the
Rockies), the Utes began applying the name *Comanche* exclusively to
them. The Ute's translation is, "One who want to fight me all the time."
Maybe a less romantic translation would be, "All time fights."

Through many years and many spellings Komántcia became Comanche. So the name comes from the Utes to the Spanish and from the Spanish to the Americans. Anyone caring to read Harston will find a different derivation. Like many of their names, *Comanche* was not of their own choosing. One of the characteristics of the snake Indians is that they all claim to be *Nerma* or *Nimma*, "The People." Apparently that was the name the Comanches had for themselves when they left Shoshone land.

When they went into Texas, they became known as Te-ich-as, or the Eater Indians. The word Te-ich-as also went through many spellings and came out Tejas. When discussing the spelling of the Comanche words as the Comanches pronounce them, Harston, who was a linguist, says that the Germans spell them the best; the English spelling is next; and the Spanish spelling is the worst.

The Comanches have been accused by some writers of having exterminated the Tejas Indians in Texas. But what seems to have happened is that over a short space of time numerous groups of the Tejas became known as Comanches. Some were Buffalo eaters, others Antelope Eaters, Fish Eaters, Dog Eaters, and Sugar Eaters, but all became known as Comanches. At this time, it would not have been proper to apply the term *tribe* to these Texas Eaters. To quote Ernest Wallace and E. Adamson Hoebel's *The Comanches: Lords of the South Plains* (Copyright 1952 by the University of Oklahoma Press, Norman):

"Tribe" when applied to the Comanches is a word of sociological but not political significance. The Comanches had a strong consciousness of kind. A Comanche, whatever his band, was a Comanche. He could say, "I am of the [Nimma]. *I am of The People.*" By dress, by speech, by thoughts and actions the Comanches held a common bond of identity and affinity that set them off from all other Indians—from all the rest of the world. In this sense, the tribe had meaning. The tribe consisted of a people who had a common way of life. But that way of life did not include political institutions or social mechanisms by which they could act as a tribal unit. There was, in the old days, no ceremonial occasion or economic enterprise that pulled all the far-flung bands together for a spell, be it ever so brief. There was no chieftain or group of chieftains to act for the tribe as a whole. There was no tribal council.

At the risk of being tedious or drawing conclusions that should be left for the reader to draw, let's assume the Nimmas did leave the neighborhood of the Shoshones in groups to make their way to the plains and southward. This would be a natural exodus, because they didn't all live in one group in the mountains. Would it not be natural for these same groups to maintain a homologous relationship in their new home or, in other words, carve out for themselves a hunting ground that would support them and then expect later comers to do the same? There was plenty of room for everyone.

I believe it will help explain their actions if we *remember they came hungry.* Apparently they quit insisting, for the time being, that they were The People and accepted the designation of *Te-ich-as,* or Eater. They must have had the heritage of hunger burned into their very marrow. And this hunger must have extended back over many generations. I think this explains their carving out of their inland empire, Comanchería, and declaring themselves the guardians of the southern herd of buffalo.

I have used the following illustration elsewhere, but it is so apt that I feel justified in using it here:

At the outbreak of the Civil War my mother's father was a plantation owner in northeastern Kentucky, in Greenup County. He worked freed Negroes. But they soon went to the towns, along with the slaves from neighboring plantations, where they knew they would be fed, without working, by the Union Army.

At this time there was plenty of Irish farm labor available—men who had fled Ireland's potato famine. The plantation was self-sustaining as far as food was concerned. But the Irish laborers could not realize that when the food heaped up in dishes on the table was exhausted there could possibly be more. Often they filled their plates to overflowing from the first dish coming to their hands. Fearing the molasses would be used up before they could empty their plates, some would even take the syrup pitcher and pour molasses over the top of their piled up food.

They couldn't conceive of barrels of molasses sitting in the cellar waiting to be used. The idea of famine and the scarcity of food was burned into their souls so deeply that this behavior went on meal after meal, day after day. My mother was nine years old when the Civil War broke out and I have the story of the hungry Irish from her. This scene forms the basis of the picture I have of the Comanche when he made his pilgrimage to the plains of Texas, and found it covered with herds of buffalo and other game. He planned never to be hungry.

Again, assuming the Comanches came to the plains hundreds of years before Hernando Cortez and his horses arrived from Spain, they probably spent generations on the trail to the south, choosing their hunting grounds. Their advancement was a matter of trial and error. They searched each day for food and water, and each winter for a place to stay. There was no Baedeker for them to turn to for guidance, no marked trails, no tourist camps.

One thing of importance we must not overlook. Directly after 1700 —I have two dates for this, 1704 and 1709—the Spanish at Santa Fe and their Indian allies set out to drive the Comanche from their midst. This was done at the request of the Utes, another Snake splinter tribe, customers of the Spaniards.

But the Comanches wouldn't be driven; they stopped the expansion of the Spanish to the north and east. Soon these northern Comanches made contact with other white men, the French, probably in what is now northeastern Oklahoma. They stopped the movement of these Frenchmen to the south and west. Both of these Comanche efforts were important to the future of the United States. Their containment of the Spanish and French took place about 90 years before Washington became President and predated the Texas Republic by 140 years and the Louisiana Purchase by roughly 100 years.

Here was an immense stretch of territory up for grabs. Had either of these two powerful European nations secured a foothold, the other would have contested it vigorously by force of arms. About this time, the Comanche became known as the Padoucas. The French so named them because it was the name used by the Kansas and Osage tribes who were Trader Chouteau's customers. Some Indian tribes called them the Iatans.

So we have two sets of names for the Comanches from the time they left their mountain homes till they settled in Oklahoma and Texas—the names they called themselves, Nerma or Nimma (The People), and Te-ich-as (Eater).

Harston, in *Comanche Land*, gives the dimensions of the Comanche empire as 650 miles east and west, and 825 miles north and south. It embraced much of Texas, parts of Kansas and Colorado, and a large part of New Mexico. Its eastern boundary followed approximately the 98th meridian through Oklahoma, thence south and east till it reached the Neches River. The line followed the Neches to the Gulf of Mexico, thence southwestward along the Gulf shore to the mouth of the Rio Grande. It followed the Rio Grande to its headwaters and then north to the Arkansas River.

Wallace and Hoebel's map of Comanchería is a bit more modest.

Their northern boundary is the same, the Arkansas River. The eastern boundary is the same to about the vicinity of Dallas; there it swings slightly west by south till it reaches the Pecos River. This river then becomes its boundary on the south and west to its headwaters, from which the boundary ran north to the Arkansas. Either area is an immense expanse of country; and until the outbreak of the Civil War, approximately, bands of Comanches, broken down into groups, subgroups, and family groups, occupied most of this territory.

An extract from the report of the Commissioner of Indian Affairs for 1869 has this to say referring to depredations in Texas: "Here lies the most unsatisfactory portion of our work. The Comanche claim, truly, that they never ceded away Texas, which was their original country, and that they therefore have a right to make war there. From the earliest settlements, they have raided upon it; killing, capturing, and stealing. . . ."

These questions insist on lurking in the back of my mind: Who were the aggressors—the newcomers? Who had owned the area, or felt they owned it, and had defended it for hundreds of years before there was a white man in the Americas? By what method of reasoning did they lose the right to live there and defend it against all comers?

Over the years, by train, horseback, mule-drawn hack, model T Ford, the "line car" that preceded the bus, and then bus, I have covered all of the territory within the boundaries drawn by Emmor Harston, excepting the immediate Great Bend country. It is a well-watered area and must have been a wonderful world for the buffalo and the Comanche. This land is real: something you can point to and say, *This is it.* So you begin to realize why the Comanche was willing to fight bitter battles to drive the Apaches from its boundaries, drive back the Mexicans, and fight the white man for 150 years, to retain possession.

When you come to the length of time the Comanche actually occupied this land and the approximate number of the tribal groups at the high tide of their successes, you are faced by human frailties and prejudices. I'm sure the Comanche fought more different people, had more enemies, and circulated over more territory than any other American Indian tribe. Few writers have grasped the true extent of Comanche activities, and most have tended to downgrade them. Especially is this true as to numbers.

One trouble of the contemporary writer was that he had come

in contact with only fragments of the tribe. The treaty-making at Medicine Lodge is an example. The only Comanches attending were the newly arrived Root Eaters and their chief, Oriter, whom the Comanches considered a Shoshone. Probably 95 percent of the tribe knew nothing of the meeting, and they wouldn't have attended, even if they had known.

Wallace and Hoebel, in their *Comanches*, write of their subject in a friendly vein, but they seem to have a blind spot when it comes to the total number of Comanches. When they give the figures of Governor Don Juan Bautista de Anza of New Mexico, who spoke of the visiting Comanches occupying 593 tepees, and those of the governor's representative, Francisco Xavier Ortiz who counted 700 lodges when he visited yet another group, Wallace and Hoebel suggest that these figures are exaggerations.

If these figures are taken at face value, and if credence is given to figures Governor Sam Houston's observers gave at a later date, an intelligent guess of 40,000 to 50,000 can be arrived at. Possibly we can make a better estimate now than could a contemporary, say in the latter part of the eighteenth century or in 1825.

Now if you take the figure of trader-agent P. L. Chouteau, who placed the number of warriors at 4,500, divide that number of Indians up over the immense area they operated in and defended, and consider all the activities they were supposed to have taken part in, you will see that they not only would have been supermen, but would have needed the help of Paul Bunyan and his Blue Ox as well. Unshod, grass-fed horses simply can't cover that much territory that fast.

Travel and communications being what they were, too often the observer was in the position of the blind men who went to see the elephant and later described what they "saw." To one who walked against the side of the elephant, the elephant was like a wall. Another, after putting his arm around one of the elephant's legs, suggested that the elephant was like a tree. One walked almost by the rear end, but did locate the tail. He insisted that the elephant was like a rope. Each reported the impression he received from the portion he touched, but none had any idea of the whole.

UNCLE SIM'S TRADING STORE

SINCE THE PEOPLE WHO SETTLED in the trade area where my father established his trading store came from just about every state and territory, their tastes and needs were as varied as their background. He located in old Faxon, that had started out as Slogan, in Comanche County, Oklahoma Territory. This was about two miles northwest of the present town of Faxon. The time was March, 1902, following the opening of the country the fall before.

Dad had no previous experience in the mercantile business. He had enjoyed several prosperous years on our farm in Marshall County, Kansas. But now he had sold his farm at an unheard-of price and was seeking two things: cheap land that would grow in value, and an easier way than farming for an old man to make a living.

We hauled the lumber for the store building from Lawton, about twenty miles to the northeast. The building's dimensions were about twenty by sixty feet, and it was of box-type construction. It was sealed, had a shingle roof, and sat on stone piers at four-foot intervals. I think the best recommendation for our construction is that these many years later it is still in use. We later moved it five miles overland to the town of Chattanooga. It stands on the main street, the oldest building in the town. I confess that it is showing its age.

Having no preconceived idea about what he should stock or exactly how a store should be run proved a decided advantage for dad. His problems were different from those facing the owner of a country store in a Kansas farming community. He had to supply the wants of people from many entirely different communities. In addition, I don't recall that we even considered that we might have Indian customers as well as white; yet we accumulated an Indian business that for probably three years actually overshadowed our white homesteader trade.

An example of the diversity of tastes, though an extreme one, is tobacco. My guess at this time is that at least eight out of ten men chewed, and many both chewed and smoked. There were five popular brands of chewing tobacco, led by Star and Horseshoe. We also carried at least ten lesser brands. Our sales of chewing tobacco, in due time, were well over one hundred pounds a week. Because we tried to satisfy everyone's taste, many people gave us their business in preference to trading at a store that carried only two or three brands, expecting their customers to take what they could get.

Duke's Mixture and Bull Durham took care of most of the cigarette smokers' needs, and about four other brands took care of the rest of the smokers. The ladies' snuff wants were not so diversified. Honest, Garrett's, and Tube Rose, each in five, ten, and twenty-five cent sizes, cared for their needs.

For the first year or so, as there was no drugstore closer than Lawton, a stock of standard drugs was a must. Generally speaking, Indian country is malaria country. Though the Indian had built up a resistance or immunity to the disease, his mosquito friends played havoc with white people coming from a nonmalarial area.

Calomel, quinine, castor oil, Grove's Chill Tonic, Black Draught, and Epsom salts were musts. Castoria and Chamberlain's were mostly for the little folks. Then of course there was need of spirits and oil of turpentine for antiseptics, camphor and oil of cloves for aching teeth, and Sloan's liniment for those who developed rheumatism. Sick horses had to have spirits of niter.

Regardless of where people came from, they could bring but little food along. Few arrived in time to get out a garden the first year, and of course there were no orchards. They could make their old clothes last over, but they had to buy food. There were lots of cattle in the country, but no butcher shops. Because there was no ice, we could get fresh meat during warm weather only when someone would butcher his animals in the hope that he could sell the meat before it spoiled.

The biggest selling meat in our store was dry-salt pork sides and bellies. People from Arkansas, the Indian Nations, and Texas were the biggest buyers of this type of meat; but many from other areas who purchased the higher-priced smoked meat at the start switched to the cheaper dry-salt before they got their claims on a make-living basis.

As I was only in the beginning of my fifteenth year and had lived all my life in one community, many things touched off my funny bone; and I had to learn to keep my face straight and roll with the punch. For instance, we had numerous people who asked for canned roasting ears, when they wanted canned corn. Others asked for a dime's worth of cheese and crackers. What they wanted was for you to cut the cheese a little short and give them some crackers to eat with it.

For some time there was no restaurant in town, and we had a table at the back of the store where people could sit and eat canned salmon, sardines, Vienna sausage, potted ham, etc. We had a few forks and spoons, a bottle of vinegar, and one of pepper sauce on the table, along with an open box of crackers. There were few hours of the day when there wasn't someone eating at the table.

We didn't have the shelf room to carry a stock of shoes. Besides, Dad did not have the kind of money it takes to carry a stock of shoes the year around. What he did was to shoe his customers twice a year. About the first of September, or a little later, we would get in several dozen pairs of shoes, for both men and women. The men's shoes were mostly of the stogy or work-shoe variety, with a few pairs of dress shoes.

We set the cases up on end at the rear of the store, took the lids off, and sold the shoes directly from the case. In a couple of weeks we would have all of our regulars shod for the winter, and only the occasional pairs left would find their way to the shelf. This scene was repeated in the spring. When we learned what kind of shoes the Indians bought for their children, especially the girls, we kept shoes in stock for them as they bought throughout the year.

We handled the bedding situation in much the same way. Dad would buy a bale of cotton blankets and a bale of cotton comforts for fall delivery, and our customers would supply their winter needs. Often we would have the whole supply sold out before the discount date ran out on the invoice.

Mother bought our piece goods, notions, and findings. She too had to feel her way. I am sure it was her taste in the selection of calicos, ginghams, and braid that was originally responsible for attracting the Indian women to our store.

It had been Dad's intention to do our own freighting. But as trade developed, freighting became too heavy a burden. He had bought a large team, wagon, and harness soon after we arrived. To get a load of stock for the store was a hard trip and a long day. He would leave early, stable and feed the team, do his running around, hitch up and load his merchandise from the several locations, and then drive the twenty miles home with a heavy load. I am sure he must have found this about as tiring as a day at harvesttime on the farm.

There was an unpleasant side to freighting besides the long days. Two creeks near our town, West Cache and Blue Beaver, had to be forded. Both of these creeks headed in the Wichita Mountains and had substantial watersheds after they left the mountains. One or both could be out of their banks, even if there had been no local rain. Freight wagons were held up for hours or days on numerous occasions. Also, it was not always possible for freight haulers to get started on the day planned.

I remember one trip when Mother went with Dad, and it rained on them nearly all the way home. Dark hit them before they got to West Cache, and they decided to come on in before the creek could rise and maroon them. Mother waded the creek and climbed the muddy bank before rejoining the wagon. It was probably eleven o'clock when they drove in. I had closed the store and gone to bed. Now I had to roll out, let them in, and care for the team; and then we had to unload the freight out of the rain. I think that was about the time Dad decided to use the regular freight haulers.

Those making their living from hauling freight were mostly men who had come into the country and registered for land. Having failed to draw a claim, and finding work with their teams plentiful, they remained. Mostly middle-aged, they had probably made other land openings before. As everyone was a stranger to everyone else, you accepted the other fellow by faith.

The merchant was dependent on the freight hauler to deposit his money for him in the bank at Lawton. Before we had been in business very long, Dad was sending around five hundred dollars a week to Lawton by the men hauling our freight. I never knew of one being unfaithful to his trust. Had he seen fit to abscond, he could have driven east to the Nations and easily had at least a thirty-six hour start on any pursuit.

Caring for the store's money was a disturbing chore. It was nearly two years before we were able to get a safe, and yet another year before we had a local bank. About the time we got our store started, Dad bought the relinquishment on an improved claim. It was about a mile and a half from the store to the house on the claim. The homesteader was returning to Texas by wagon, so he sold us his furniture as well. When we began living on the claim, it meant carrying the money back and forth.

As it was always dark, winter or summer, before we could close the store, we worked various and sundry schemes to get the money back and forth. It was my job to hitch up the team, as well as to carry the silver. We could easily have two to three hundred dollars in silver if the freight wagons had been held up a day or two.

After I had tied the team out front, I would continue working around the store, including making necessary trips out to the tent warehouse in the rear. Finally I would stroll out into the darkness and not come back. I would have the coin sacks, my shotgun, and my bird dog. I tried to go a little different route each night; and before I approached the house I would send the dog ahead to inspect the house and barn to see if we had any company.

Mother handled the paper money and checks. She had a brownish tan wallet like the ones men carried in their inside coat pockets in those days. It was about the color of mesquite grass, and she had several feet of black thread fastened to it. She planned, if anyone stopped her, to throw the wallet out into the prairie. The thread would help us find it the next morning.

Our Indian business just seemed to happen. At least we had made no conscious effort to attract it. In fact, Dad and Mother never made any effort to learn the Comanche language. We were surprised to learn later that many merchants made it a practice to boost the price if an Indian was buying. I am sure that idea never occurred to any of us. We were later to find that the missionaries had been checking our prices and bookkeeping and had passed the word on to the Indians that we had one price for all.

We had no family history of past trouble with Indians; so when an Indian came in the store we accorded him the same degree of courtesy that we did a white person, and the Indians responded. In due time some of the Indians wanted credit until Grass Money payment time. The government paid fifty dollars twice a year to each man, woman, and child. This represented interest on tribal funds the government was holding in trust.

Carrying the Indians' accounts until Grass Money time brought on an unlooked-for complication. We had naturally supposed that when they received their pay, the Indians would return to their allotments. But the campout on the reservation of hundreds of families was too much like the old tribal life for them to return readily to their lonesome allotment camp.

They could feast, visit, gamble, and hold horse races, and those that drank were supplied by the whiskey peddlers. Then too there were many visitors from other tribes, as they knew food, beef, and whiskey would be plentiful.

To get our money we had to go to the reservation and collect while they still had it. They were pleased to see us, and they paid readily. They wanted to keep their credit good, but putting aside the necessary amount so as to pay up on their return was too much planning for them. That was especially true of the drinkers.

My first collection trip was successful and uneventful, and from then on it was my regular chore, and an interesting one. I would be gone from one to two days if the payment was held near the town of Cache, and longer when it was held near Ft. Sill at what was called "The Stone Store."

When death struck our little community, we were poorly prepared. Two women and one baby died in a single night. All the needs for a funeral were lacking—no undertaker, no caskets, no cemetery, and no preacher.

Early the next morning caskets were put together from yellow pine and brought to our store and set on sawhorses. There the townswomen covered, padded, and lined them. Black calico was used for the covering of the adult caskets, and white muslin for the baby's. Quilting cotton was used for the padding and pillow, and bleached muslin for the lining.

Handles intended for toolboxes were screwed on the sides of the adult caskets by Dad after the women had tacked the black calico in place. Permission to bury the bodies on the claim adjoining the town on the north was granted by an old German homesteader.

Mary Armstrong, a twenty-year-old girl, whose previous religious participation had been confined to Epworth League, conducted the services. She would be called on again and again for like duty before the Methodist circuit rider (he used a bicycle) would find us, and a number of homemade caskets would be brought to our store for the women to make presentable. But this was the only time there was more than one casket in the store at a time.

Twenty-one miles and back, and the fording of two creeks, meant eleven hours of hard driving by a good team and lumber wagon. That was too long a delay in warm weather to put away a body. One who lived in those times understands what Matt Dillon meant when he told Chester to find a shovel.

The busiest day of the store's history was preceded by a norther that had struck in the night, and it was blowing icy rain in little scuds or showers, one behind the other, the next day. There hadn't been a customer in the store all morning. Then about ten o'clock the little Indian wagons began to arrive in town. By the time the first dozen or so of the little prairie schooners had arrived, they had all the hitchracks in town occupied.

Those who came later pulled up on the grass, unhitched, and tied their horses to the rear wheels. Soon our store was filled until the only vacant space was behind the counters. These were strange Indians, and were not from our trade territory. They were from the north and west, along the south side of the mountains. They were on their way to a medicine ground on the south side of Red River. Nearly all of them were in their second day's journey, and they were still two full days from the medicine ground. It is possible our Indians had started the day before.

Whether they had planned to rendezvous in our town, or whether they just happened to buy supplies there, I will never know. Anyhow they not only bought all our staple groceries, but, because of the weather, they stripped us of bedding, underwear, socks, stockings, and the few shoes we had in stock.

It must have been three o'clock before the Indians' wants were satisfied and they began to hitch up and leave. In an hour or so our town was as empty as it was when we drove in that morning. Many of the shelves were bare to the wall. But we now had time to take a long breath, to try to bring order out of chaos, and to find something for our empty stomachs. Mine, at least, was demanding attention.

Soon after our store was built, Dad was appointed justice of the peace. I have no recollections of why, or how, if I ever knew. Anyhow it happened. He was the only magistrate from Lawton, twenty miles to the northeast, to Frederick, twenty-six miles to the west and south. Likewise, he was about center between Cache on the north and Red River to the south.

He tried a few cases involving stock damage to crops by loose herds of horses and cattle, but his principal business came when drunk cowboys, or would-be cowboys, tried to take the town apart. The town had no police force, so unless there happened to be a deputy sheriff in town, or Indian police, Dad would have to deputize some citizens and order them to quell the disturbance and bring in the offenders.

The nearest thing to a jail the town possessed was a community " 'fraid-hold" or cave. Obstreperous drunks were thrown in there to sober up. The most amusing incident of this kind involved an old fellow that bragged he had been a member of Quantrill's Raiders and an associate of Jesse James and Cole Younger. One night he was playfully trying to cut a barber's throat by sawing his neck up and down on the edge of a broken saloon window, and he was arrested by one of Dad's civilian posses. A young slim-jim of a chap was arrested with him. They were obviously too drunk to be tried, so Dad ordered them put in the cave to sober up.

When anyone was put in the cave, logs were piled on the door to hold them in. We hadn't moved to the claim yet, and Dad and Mother slept on a folding bed in the back of the store. I had a cot up front, between the counters. About two o'clock there was a knock on the back door. Our two drunks were hunting a place to stay all night. By a coincidence, they had come to the judge that had ordered them thrown into the cave.

Dad never let on. They had been so drunk they had no memory of him. He got up and fixed them a bed out in the tent wareroom, and they were grateful to him for the favor. Quite early the next morning, two members of the posse were at the store, badly put out that their prisoners had escaped. They said the slim one, who needed but a small hole, had dug his way up beside the stairway with a pocket knife, rolled off the logs, and let the larger and older man out.

Dad let them stew a while and then told them their prisoners were safely in his custody, but he would let them sleep as late as they wished. Maybe they would sleep until court time. The prisoners didn't sleep quite that late, but they were badly surprised when he told them to return to the store for trial after they had eaten their breakfast.

One of the provisions of the law under which this land had been opened was that Civil War veterans and their widows could register by mail. Evidently a large number of veterans and widows so registered, for many drew claims in our area. Most of them drew pensions of eight dollars per month, which was tops at that time. They were paid every three months and had to file for it each time. Dad always filled out their papers free, including the notary fee of twenty-five cents, and he was truly a popular person at filing time.

As nearly as I recall, all of them, veterans and widows alike, were accompanied by a son, or daughter and son-in-law. Several of the old girls smoked little clay pipes, and whenever one of them showed up, Dad turned his tobacco poke over to them. They always sat back by the stove to smoke, winter or summer, and I have seen as many as three of them at one time smoking up a storm with Dad's tobacco.

Most of the veterans, and all the widows, were several years older than Dad, but nearly every one of them called him Uncle Sim. In due time that was the only name you ever heard anyone call him.

In 1908 the store lost its attraction for Dad, though it was prospering and had grown in volume of business each year. He decided to retire. He traded the store for land to a farmer who wanted to turn merchant, just as Dad had a few years before.

THE LOST ONES

~~~~~~~~~~~~~~~~~~~~~~~~~~~~~~~~~~~~~~

WHEN WE WENT into the Comanche country in the spring of 1902, it was not only a new country but a new way of life to me, a fourteen-year-old Kansas farm boy. The people I met, homesteaders or home-seekers, came from nearly every state in the Union, as well as from the Indian Nations. Ringed about us were Comanche families, camped rather than living on their allotments.

It was the Comanches, of course, who made the greatest impression on me. Almost as soon as Dad got his trading store opened, we started having an Indian trade. It just seemed to happen. We made no conscious effort to attract the Indians and wouldn't have known how had we wanted to try.

Mother bought our opening stock of dry goods, and she continued to do the buying as long as we ran the store. A few bolts of bright colors, in both calico and gingham, together with matching cotton braid, possibly proved an attraction to the Indian women at the start. Then too, Dad and Mother had the theory that we should treat everyone with the same degree of courtesy. These two things were the only concessions, if they were concessions, you could say we made.

Another thing that probably helped was that a missionary who ran a mission back to the northeast on Blue Beaver Creek made a check, unbeknownst to us, of the prices we charged to the white and

25

the Indian customers. Later he ran another check on the accuracy of our bookkeeping. He passed this information on to the Indians. I can well remember my embarrassment when one day, after he had finished his investigations, the Reverend Mr. Deyo shook my hand and thanked me for "dealing honestly with my people." It seemed just a little hard for him to understand that a white merchant would voluntarily deal honestly with the Indians. But I am sure Dad, Mother, and I would have been just as puzzled had anyone suggested we deal any other way. At least, I never heard the subject discussed.

I am positive that at the time I had never heard the word "romantic," but it represents the way I thought about the Comanches in our trade territory. They belonged to the group known as Quohadie Tejas, or Antelope Eaters. Their range had been the high plains, centered in what is now the Texas Panhandle, and their leader was Quanah Parker. They had fought at Adobe Walls and in June, 1876, had been the last of the Comanches to surrender to the Army. By simple arithmetic, I knew that every male from the late forties upward had been a warrior. For my own convenience in thinking of them, I separated them into a group I called "the old fellows."

There was another group I didn't have to separate out, those ranging in age from their late teens to the late thirties or early forties. They separated themselves out. Not only did they hold themselves aloof from the whites, but there was a separateness between them and the older Indians—apparently including their own parents.

I learned that these particular Indians had been East to a school financed by the government at Carlisle, Pennsylvania. I learned that most of them had the equivalent of a high school education, and some had done college work. Now that they were home with the tribe, they made not the slightest move to use what they had learned, either to better their own condition or to be of assistance to the tribe.

They talked only Comanche among themselves, and wouldn't speak English when conversing with whites if they could make themselves understood by grunts, sign language, or pointing. I called these Indians the Carlisle group.

These young men and older boys, as well as the girls of the same age group, were better-looking Indians than the older, warrior-aged group and their squaws. It was most noticeable in their legs, which were straighter and better developed and appeared longer—the bandy look of the oldsters' legs had disappeared. These young Indians had spent less time on horseback and more time inside, out of the weather; nor had they ever ridden the war trails. The women of this group took better care of their hair. The older women's hair generally had an untidy look.

This sullen aloofness and aimless drifting didn't affect the younger children—it seemed to set in when a boy got to be fifteen or sixteen years old. The younger children, when they arrived home on vacation, were bursting with energy. They rode their ponies helter-skelter over the prairies and rivaled the channel cat in Cache Creek with their cavorting, swimming, and diving.

They came to town with their parents—the girls riding in a hack or the little lumber wagon with the women. If it was the wagon, the bows and canvas cover converted it into a little prairie schooner. On a nice day the canvas would be rolled up a ways on either side, to let the air through.

Comanche men and boys never rode in the wagon or hack with the women. The boys would be riding along with their father, horseback. If there were not enough stock saddles to go around, the younger boys would be riding ancient Mexican-type saddles. These Mexican saddles had a flat look, compared to the up-to-date stock saddle. Neither the fork nor the cantle was as high, while the seat was broader. Its most distinguishing feature was the top of the fork. Thin, broad, and round, it made one think of a pancake. I am sure the tops of some of the horns were as much as four inches across.

Somehow, the youngsters always had a few nickels to spend for candy, cakes, and wax—their name for all kinds of chewing gum. The happy parents stood around and glowed in their pride. Sometimes the parents had one of the youngsters show off—they would have one of the boys interpret as they bought their groceries or other store items. They wanted everyone in the store to see how much their children had learned.

But all this youthful, happy exuberance suddenly vanished in the late teens. Few of the girls stayed in school as long as the boys, and the girls never got the good from their Carlisle clothes. About the second or third time they came to the store after their last year in school, they would buy some gay-colored, patterned calico along with matching cotton braid. The next time you saw them, they would be wearing a *pit-si-qui-na.*

The young men did wear out their white man's clothes, but seemingly remembered none of the white man's ways. And they seemed to have forgotten the old tribal ways as well.

In my thinking, I found it convenient to put the women and girls in yet another group. One of the first things I learned was the taboo which prevented women and girls from talking to men, Indians or white, other than their own menfolks, excepting on the most necessary occasions. Because of this I never addressed them unless they spoke to me.

I was consciously making every effort to learn as much of the language as I could, and in time I was able to catch on quickly to what the men were talking about and to follow their conversation. But the women seemed to have a vocabulary of their own. I would often listen to a group of women talking in the store, or out in the camp, but I could distinguish only an occasional word.

Those who conceived of educating the Indian youths also conceived the idea that the educating must be done in faraway places, and little has been done through the years to change the practice. Even as I type this article, several hundred Indian children from New Mexico, Arizona, and other western states are attending Chilocco Indian School in northern Oklahoma.

While in Carlisle or other Indian boarding schools, Indian children had slept in clean beds with sheets changed every week. They had sat in chairs at a table with a clean tablecloth and had eaten food served from clean dishes. They had been taught the use of the knife, fork, and spoon. But when the Indian boy arrived home for good, he had only his parents' camp to go to. Though the Comanche families were living on their allotments, they continued to live a camp life, much the same as they had lived the previous twenty-five years as Reservation Indians.

In this camp our Carlisle graduate sat on the ground, or a log, or a goods box. He ate his food from a pie tin and was served directly from the kettle in which the food had been cooked. If a boy was lucky, he had a fork and spoon to go along with his pocketknife as eating utensils.

Spring, summer, and fall they all slept in the brush arbor on platforms and under seldom-washed cotton blankets. When the northers became blue and came with regularity, they slept in conventional tents, either on the ground or on low platforms constructed with poles. Once in a while, as I rode on my collection trips, I would see a set of tepee poles, twenty-two in number, left from the old days. Now they were covered with canvas.

The government had built a small box house, generally fourteen by twenty-eight feet, at most family camps, but it could hardly accommodate the multiple-wife family, still in vogue. Mostly it was the camp's storage house, an out-of-the-weather place for saddles, harness, horse feed and medicine, and the women's sewing machine.

I almost never knew one of the Carlisle Comanches, man or boy, to take a job. There were riding jobs on the ranches, and many merchants would have been glad to hire a Comanche clerk. Old Indians with horse herds were forced to hire white broncobusters to break their horses. I asked an Indian father once, in my ignorance, why he was paying to have his horses ridden, and added the naïve qestion, "Don't your boys like to break horses to ride?" In our Scottish household I had never heard the words tact and diplomacy.

The old fellow gave a snort of disgust and replied, partly in sign language and partly in words, "They more like riding sitting-down-walking," that is to say, riding a bicycle.

The question had been crude on my part, and I should have been pulled up short for my brashness. But I was all excited, thinking what a wonderful lot of fun it would be to gentle and ride those ponies. I had actually helped do it on the farm with wild horses from Oregon. I knew there was a better way to break a horse to ride than to throw a saddle on a wild horse, climb on, and spur him until he was exhausted from bucking.

Just a little time spent gentling a horse pays big dividends. Let him wear a saddle while he is tied snugly to a post or in a stall. Then, when you first ride him do not use your spurs. We first taught a horse to lead while wearing a saddle. Then, the first few times we rode him we had someone on a strong, gentle horse keep the wild horse's head snubbed close to the other's saddle horn and lead him.

Indian boys had nothing but time. Tribal custom had been to require no menial tasks from boys as they grew up: "Pretty soon be warrior, may-be-so die." But in the old days, the boy was expected to work with the horses, herd them, learn to train them, and become an expert horseman. From my observations, the Carlisle boys were interested in horses only when they wanted to ride somewhere. Had they seen fit to gentle and break their fathers' horses, they would have had much more salable animals.

By the time the settlers moved in, the antelope had disappeared from the Comanche country, as well as the deer and turkey. As early as we arrived, I never saw a turkey. Some of the small black bear held out in the Wichita mountains for a few years. But there was no possible chance for the Indian to live on large game.

Ducks, geese, plover, curlew, snipe, bobwhite, and prairie chickens were plentiful, and West Cache Creek was teeming with channel cat, blue and yellow cat, and perch; yet I never saw an Indian hunting birds or dangling a hook in the water.

Fish-eating, I was to learn later, was almost taboo. Wallace and Hoebel, doing research for their Comanche history, gained the impression that the Comanches ate fish only to keep from actually starving. They had no objection to white people's fishing in their streams. I fished for miles up and down West Cache Creek, and no one ever objected.

I have often thought if I owned a farm West Cache ran through, I would charge people just to look at the creek. To the eye of a boy, there was nothing so beautiful as the blue-green water running over the slightly reddish-tinted granite sand. There was no quicksand on West Cache. Its sand was so sharp you scarcely sank in it when you walked, nor did you rile the water. Here and there were small beaches of clean sand where the swimmer could enter and leave the water. This cool, clear water came from the Wichita Mountains. Strong, vigorous elms along the high banks furnished shade for the swimmer or fisherman. More than sixty years later, I still feel it was the most beautiful prairie stream I have ever seen.

Too young in those days to realize the cause, I couldn't help but sense the terrible separateness between my Carlisle group and the older men and women. Later I was to realize that government educators of the late nineteenth century, in carrying out their theory of educating young Indians, violated the unwritten bedrock commandment of human behavior: "Thou shalt not speak ill of any man in the presence of his offspring." You must not cut away the support from beneath his feet. You may be able to furnish him another platform, on which he may see fit to step; but he can never step onto your platform if you have first destroyed his footing.

Even the Comanche children's language became taboo at Carlisle. After drilling into the children's minds what terrible people their par-

ents were, the teachers continued to accent the differences between
the parents' behavior and what would be expected of the children
when they left school. Dinning this into the children's ears for a dozen
years or so without further plans for the future, the teachers sent them
back to these same parents. Pride of parentage, pride of tribe, pride
of language had been either destroyed or so badly weakened and erod-
ed that the young Indian had nothing to step from with confidence.

Instead of seeking to make a place for himself, aiding his parents
and tribe by using his training and education, the Carlisle Indian
moved into his parents' camp. There, without self-respect and certainly with no hope for betterment lying ahead, he contented himself with
living on his meager Grass Money and what lease money his allotment
brought in, when and if it was rented.

At that time an agriculture lease brought in only $1.25 per acre, or
$200 per year. In addition to the $200, the government required the
lessee, as further compensation over the first five-year period, to fence
the allotment with a four-wire fence with posts every rod, to break
out a certain number of acres of sod for crops, to build a fourteen by
twenty-eight box house with a shingle roof, and to dig and wall up a
well at least forty feet deep, unless plentiful water was found at a
lesser depth. Grass leases brought even less.

Land along the streams had been chosen by the Comanches for
their allotments, and this gave them a monopoly on water, wood, and
bottomland. Those with land along West Cache and Post Oak creeks
also had a fine grade of sand to sell. These 160-acre tracts, one for
each man, woman, and child living on a certain date in 1901, were
the remnant of the millions of acres these Indians' forefathers had
roamed over and ruled for many, many centuries.

No one expected the old ones to change their ways so radically as
to try to learn to farm. But it was beyond my boyish understanding
why the younger Indians fresh from school, some even with college
rating, didn't try farming. Many of them had first class sandy-loam
bottomland. They could look around them and see white families
making a living on their upland farms, putting out orchards, and
even adding a room to their houses now and then.

I discovered in time that a number of the old fellows were really
going out of their way to be nice to me, and in lost pup fashion I
responded. I thought little of it at the time, and took these friendships in my stride. Maybe I thought of them as my due. It wasn't

until years later, after I had gone away to college myself, that I tried to analyze the reasons for the old fellows' interest in me.

One conclusion I reached was that because of my size and what they saw me doing, they had thought of me as being older than I actually was. I was as tall as I am now and weighed a muscular 180 pounds. My parents were expecting a man's work from me, and they saw to it that I kept busy. In my skills, I could do a man's work and was doing it, though I was carrying around on my large body only a fourteen-year-old head and, of course, a like amount of experience.

While we were getting the store into operation, Dad hired the team and me out several days to haul rock for the new school's foundation. Then, to have some spending money, I hired myself out to a farmer to break prairie sod—driving one of his teams. I hauled freight for the store, waited on the trade, and, after Dad bought a relinquishment, did the necessary farm work on the claim. When I had leisure I fished and hunted. These old fellows often saw me five or more miles from town, and to the horse-minded Comanches that was an unheard-of distance for anyone to walk.

This continuous activity of mine must have contrasted bitterly with the inertness of their own offspring. And one other possibility occurred to me. Almost all the older Comanches drank hard liquor, when the opportunity was present, but they had great respect for any white man who abstained.

Here was a man who could obtain whiskey at any time and yet didn't drink. It meant something special to them. In their book I was a Jesus Man. Apparently they could conceive of no other reason for abstention. This thinking possibly related to the missionaries, sent out by churches in the East, who were the only white men they had come in contact with who didn't drink.

One Carlisle man who found a beneficial and happy use for his education was Charley Ross. He must have been one of the very first Comanches sent to Carlisle after the surrender in 1876. A happy, outgoing chap, he made a life's work of smoothing the way between the white man and the older Indians. I saw him often and knew him quite well while Dad had his trading store. Once I saw him interpreting a sermon at an Indian camp meeting. After I started to practice law in Oklahoma City, I saw him acting as an interpreter in court trials, and once in a legislative committee hearing. He was always available when his people needed him.

One afternoon in the late 1930s I drove into the little town of Faxon on business for a client. When I got out of the car, I was face to face with Charley Ross. It had been long since I had talked with him, and my happiness at meeting him appeared to be matched by his at seeing me. For a Plains Indian he was truly an old man—somewhere in his seventies. We sat down on the running board of the car, and dusk found us still sitting there. I had forgotten I had a client, and Charley had forgotten that the daughter with whom he lived would be worried about his being out in the raw, chilly evening air.

I had it in mind to ask him many questions about himself, other questions about old Comanche friends of whom I had lost track, and yet other questions about Comanches in general. But he too had questions, and insistent ones. He knew I had become a lawyer, of course, but mostly he wanted to know about my children—for what place in life they had fitted themselves.

When he learned that my oldest son was already a lawyer and the younger son was preparing for law school, he grinned with pleasure. My father was the first magistrate appointed after the opening, and his jurisdiction had stretched for twenty or more miles in any direction. To Charley that meant Dad had been learned in the law. Then I had followed in the law profession, and now two sons were following me. To Charley, this progression was wonderful.

He was equally pleased to match up my daughters with his. My oldest was on the faculty of a small college, and the younger was teaching in a high school. Both his daughters were teachers and had married teachers.

Another Carlisle product who launched himself into the white man's life stream and kept himself afloat was one of Quanah Parker's sons. But then, he had a motive. He was in love.

Chief Quanah Parker's house was about three miles from the little town of Cache, Oklahoma. Some Texas cattlemen had settled him in a kind of apartment house just south of the Wichita Mountains, where West Cache Creek breaks out into the prairie. He was recognized by the government as chief of the Comanches. Like all the older Indians married to more than one wife, he had been allowed to keep his four or five remaining wives. One son was a Methodist minister, one daughter was married to a minister, and two other daughters married well-to-do white men.

The father of the Carlisle son's sweetheart had been a missionary to the Comanches. The girl told young Parker that if it was his intention to live around Cache, become another Carlisle loafer, and bask in the reflection of his father's glory, she wasn't interested. But if he was willing to go away and live where people had never heard of the Comanches or of Quanah Parker, she would marry him.

Quanah's son agreed to leave Oklahoma, and they married and moved to Florida. The one thing young Parker could think of that he would have the nerve to try was driving a baggage wagon. So they bought a team and a light dray, and he began hauling baggage and making light deliveries. He made a living from the start, and in time built a first-class transfer business.

But Charley Ross and Quanah Parker's son were exceptions. As a lawyer in Oklahoma City I saw a number of pitiable incidents in the courts, in which Indians who couldn't catch hold of the new life were testifying through an interpreter. I know they had been sent to government schools, but they preferred to pretend they didn't know English, rather than to accept the responsibilities of their training. They wished to be thought of as belonging to an older generation that had been denied advantages.

The educated young women, too, fell into the dull, dawdling existence led by their men, although I did know two girls, just out of school, who married industrious white men and became hard-working wives, and whose unions prospered financially. (Comanche wives, by the way, seldom bore more than two children, and often only one. But mixed marriages, particularly those of a white man and a Comanche woman, produced fruitfully.)

One episode illustrates the attitude of most of the educated women. We had been operating the store several months, and I was proud of my good trade vocabulary. I knew the Comanche name for almost everything in the store that might interest the Indians, and I know their names and designations of money. One day, however, I was neither making myself understood by a very old squaw nor understanding what she was trying to tell me.

The ancient one's patience wore thin, and I am sure the line of chatter flowing from her withered lips in a stream was not complimentary to either my intelligence or my ancestry. Then I was suddenly rescued by a pleasant-faced, nice-mannered young Comanche woman on whom I had waited many times. "She wants coffee," she told me in perfect English.

This was the first time I had heard this woman say more than a single word of English at a time. When she had bought coffee from me, she had asked for *"to-o-pac."* (I believe the Comanches have three names for coffee, but this one, meaning "black water," is the only one I remember.) And she had gone through her whole grocery list the same way. It had been *"pina"* for "sugar four bits," *"hocoon"* for "matches five cents," *"mo-be-po-dra"* for "dry salt meat six bits." Or maybe she would point to canned corn and ask, *"Heepet?"* or "How much?" She had always asked for one article at a time, and paid for it before asking for the next item. Though she had been educated at Carlisle, she had consistently played the part of an uneducated blanket squaw.

Even living as close to the Comanches as I did, I never heard any of them mention the experiences of the children who were sent away to school—say in the late 1870s, when Charley Ross must have gone. This was another of the things I remember having failed to ask him. Then by chance I heard a Pueblo woman speak out on the subject.

She appeared to be about fifty, and she ran a small souvenir shop in the Taos Pueblo. She dressed as a white woman shopkeeper might have dressed, and her hair was tastefully arranged. She used excellent English, and a lady in our sightseeing party, curious about her appearance and her fine command of the language, asked, "Did you attend a white school?"

This is the Indian woman's answer, as nearly word for word as I can give it. "Fifty years ago this fall—I was about five or six years old —a great number of white men came to this Pueblo one day. We didn't know what these men wanted, nor who they were. Some wore badges of the United States marshals, and we were to learn others were from the Indian schools. There were some Indian police, but not of our people.

"They didn't speak to anyone. They told no one why they had come. Suddenly a large number of them began to make a house-to-house search, and the rest stayed on guard in the Plaza. As they went through the houses, they seized every child from about five up to fourteen or fifteen. Screaming and crying, we children were dragged one by one out into the middle of the plaza. They herded us there as though we were a bunch of wild cattle. No one knew what was wrong —neither we children nor our parents.

"We were all screaming and crying hysterically. I had seen white men but had never spoken to one. I had a great fear of them. They kept us in a circle, with our parents on the outside, and we couldn't run to them for comfort. As I sobbed and cried, I became aware that someone was talking to me—calling me by name—talking loud in our tongue.

"I began looking around, and it was my grandfather. He was a very old man, and he stood back away from the circle of white men and didn't look toward us children. He didn't want the white men to know he was talking to one of us, and neither our white guards nor the Indian ones knew our tribal language.

"He talked loud, so I would hear him above the screaming and crying of the other children. 'Daughter, the white man is all-powerful!' he shouted. 'There is nothing we can do to help you. They are going to take you away and put you in school. They won't really harm you. They want to teach you the white man's way. Should you run away, they will catch you, bring you back, and punish you.

"'There is a way you can defeat the white man. Learn everything well he tries to teach you. Learn everything about the white man's way. Learn to speak his language. Then you will have defeated the white man. You will be as wise as he in the white man's way; and he won't like it because you will know also the Indian's way.'

"I stopped my sobbing. I stood as straight as my old, old grandfather, and I did as he told me. I learned to speak the white man's language without accent, and I have had a better education than most white people. I mastered every course they offered me. I was always properly behaved and they treated me well. I was able to help many Indian children adjust to the white man's school. But never have I forgiven the white man for the brutal way they rounded up us children and separated us from our parents.

"They had not let our parents know they were coming for us. Had our parents known, they said they would have taken us to the mountains, where no one would ever find us."

Similar roundups must have taken place among the Comanches in the early Reservation period—the late seventies, the early eighties, maybe into the nineties. They could even have used the army. It was handy, there at Fort Sill. It was Indian Bureau policy—an unfortunate policy forced upon a people with thousands of generations of freedom and independence behind them.

In my time there were older brothers and sisters who had traveled the school trail and who softened the emotional jolt on the little ones. But it must still have been a terrible shock for any young child to be taken from his camp home and hauled by hack and train to faraway places, there to be tossed neck and heels into the white man's way of life and forced to eat his food . . . sleep alone in bed . . . and learn life from his books.

POLYGAMY IN COMANCHE COUNTRY

MY CURIOSITY concerning polygamy had been thoroughly honed for some two years before I learned that our family was going to the Comanche country. For lack of other reading material, I was reading the newspapers from front to back at a very early age. The *Kansas City Star* published a weekly *Star* and a weekly *Journal.* (The R.F.D. was still a couple of years away, and living in the country as we did there was no object in our taking a daily newspaper.)

It seemed that a man had been elected to the U.S. Senate who because of his religious connections was suspected of having more than one wife. Both the *Star* and the *Journal* gave a great deal of space to the possibility that we had an actual practicing polygamist in the Senate. Likewise both papers carried a column or two, each issue, of comments by the readers. Polygamy was entirely new to me, and I read every word of the articles and the comments from readers. The slant of both articles and letters was strictly antipolygamy. They uniformly drew a picture of something that was seen as soul-destroying and reprehensible.

This storm had scarcely run its course before the opening of the Kiowa-Comanche country caught my interest, as my parents planned to move there. Now I was searching the papers for every mention of the Indian country. Quanah Parker seemed to be the Indian with the greatest influence, and the *Star* and *Journal* had a story of some sort about him in nearly every issue.

They ranged from the story about his white mother's having died of a broken heart when she was captured and returned to her own people, to stories about his physical prowess and his ability as a leader—about how, when once he had led his braves into Fort Sill under arms and surrendered, he had turned his attention to being a leader in peace. Then there was much said of how he had become a business adviser to other southwestern tribes. All in all, the stories painted a picture of a versatile and dedicated leader.

Two of these stories made me aware that the Comanches practiced polygamy. One had to do with the decision of some Texas cattlemen, who had been renting Indian grass from Quanah, that he should have a house. They hauled the lumber from Wichita Falls. They had to ford it across the Red River's quicksand and drag it through the mud of high-banked Deep Red, a total of fifty-five miles as the crow flies, to a site three and a half miles from where the town of Cache now stands, and on the west bank of West Cache Creek. The house could be considered an apartment house. Each of Quanah's wives had an apartment. In addition, there was a general living area.

The other story that stands out in my memory had to do with the Indian Department's efforts to do away with polygamy before the white people actually moved in and set up local government on a county level. Once this was done, everyone would be subject to the Oklahoma territorial law.

The department pinned its hopes on winning over Quanah Parker, the last war leader of the Comanches. Not only was he respected by the Comanches, but he had become a sort of bellwether to the other Indians involved in this opening—the Kiowas, Caddos, Wichitas, and Apaches.

As the department considered this a very minor issue, its officials apparently approached Quanah Parker casually on the subject. They simply explained that the new officers of the local communities would have to arrest any Indian with more than one wife, just as they would have to arrest any white man found with multiple wives.

The solution, they said, was very simple. All the Indian had to do was pick out the wife he wanted to keep and then explain to the others that under white man's law they were surplus and would have to move elsewhere. "You see," they went on plausibly, "if they choose to live on their allotment, the department will fence it and build them a little house. Every six months they will have their Grass Money for living expenses, and they can also lease out their allotment to a white man to farm.

Now Quanah had a question: "How is the Indian to tell which wife to keep and which is surplus?"

"That's easy," the department's spokesman answered. "Keep the one you love the best, the one you have had the longest, maybe the one that has borne you the most children, perhaps the prettiest one, or even the youngest and strongest. Since you can have but one, select the one you want to keep, and tell the rest to go."

It is always well to remember that the Comanches considered themselves as "The People" and were never awed in any company. In addition Chief Parker was proud of the fact that his white mother came from one of the first families of Texas, and I doubt that he ever felt inferior to any man. His reply not only shocked the government men, but sent them scurrying around for another answer to the question.

I think Quanah Parker's answer reached an all-time high in negotiating: "I have had a number of wives. Sometimes a wife dies and I take another to replace her. Once I had seven wives, but now I have only five. Each of my wives I have for a different length of time. Some I have for a very long time. Some for a very short time. I love all my wives equally. I could not call my wives together and tell them, 'Now that the white man is coming, his law says that I can keep but one wife.

" 'White man says I should keep the one that I love best. The rest are surplus and must go and live somewhere else. So this is the woman I love the best, and the rest of you are surplus. You must go and live elsewhere.' This I cannot do. You come to my house. You pick out a wife for me to keep. Then you tell 'em."

This ended the idea of telling Comanche wives that any of them were surplus. There is little doubt that any negotiator suggesting to any Comanche wife that she was surplus would have lived only as long as it took the squaw to cover the distance between them and to use her butcher knife. Nor would the three troops of cavalry stationed at Fort Sill have made any headway in quelling the squaw uprising.

Once Quanah Parker convinced the Indian Department officials that it would be impossible to handle the multiple wife situation as simply as the department heads had imagined, the department and Chief Parker arrived at this sensible solution:

Nothing would be done about men who already had more than one wife, but they were not to take any more wives. Even if one died, a man would have to get along on what wives he had left. All single men would be restricted to marrying one wife. A violation of any one of these restrictions would bring about prosecution under the white man's law.

Among the Indians I knew intimately enough to be familiar with their family lives, I knew of only one who violated this agreement. He was a compulsive drinker, and was about to starve the two-wife family he already had when he took on a third wife. Ultimately he had to move onto the reservation permanently so as to get food, and I lost track of him. His Indian neighbors seemed to be ashamed of his conduct and tried to ignore his existence.

Polygamy had been an economic and social necessity for the Comanches. From the time they entered written history, when they came into contact with the Spanish people of Santa Fe about 1700, until their surrender in 1876 at Fort Sill, their history was one of continuous warfare. They had fought and defeated the Pawnees, the Osages, the Tonkawas, the Navahoes, the Utes, and the Pueblo Indians in New Mexico and Arizona. They had established an inland empire, Comanchería, just as legitimately as Charlemagne established his, and for a time they rode the crest of the horse-buffalo culture. They marketed horses with the Canadian Indians, raided as much as 1,500 miles into Mexico, and had seen the Pacific Ocean. They had stopped the advance of Spain to the north and to the east and that of the French to the west and to the south. Then, in the years of the new kind of warfare which brought about their decline, the United States, the Republic of Texas, the Confederacy, and Mexico were among their enemies. During all this time there was no period when the tribe as a whole was at peace.

In war men die young, and the male-female balance is lost. Continual warfare brought about an erosion of the numbers of Comanche men out of all proportion to the natural losses, through death, of the women. It was only through the custom of polygamy that every woman could have a husband and the birthrate could be maintained.

Then too, there had to be many trained hands to keep a Comanche camp functioning properly. The tasks were varied and time-consuming, and no one woman could have taken care of all of them.

The warrior-husband was the killer of game, the procurer of buffalo meat, the Comanches' principal source of food. He had to have two sets of trained horses—one trained for war, the other for the killing of buffalo. In either pursuit, his life was largely dependent on the horse. He manufactured both his riding gear and his weapons, and he trained his own horses. His fighting was practically on a twelve-month basis, since, though the Comanches did not like winter fighting, most of the ambitious warriors made raiding expeditions into Old Mexico when the group went into winter camp.

The husband, therefore, could be of little or no help around the camp, and the labor had to be divided among the women. Usually one of the women was an expert horsewoman and had the responsibility of her husband's horse herd, which often numbered a hundred or more. When the fall hunt was on for the winter's supply of meat, the wives did the skinning and butchering. They dried the meat and made the pemmican. Also, they prepared and tanned the hides. After the tanning came the making of clothing. This included everything the family wore, both in summer and winter. Since there was neither needle nor thread, the holes in the leather were made with a stone awl or one made from bone, and sinew taken from along the backbone of a buffalo or deer was used for thread.

Other hides were converted into robes for bedding or into covers for the tepees. When camp was moved, tepees had to be taken down and fastened on travoises, like all the other camp gear, and then camp must be set up again at the new location. All of this was strictly woman's work.

Somewhere, sometime, during breathing spells from all these duties, the women bore babies, nursed them, and raised them to be good Comanches. And all this was in a society without a recognized medium of exchange, in which no one could hire anything done. The Comanches did, however, utilize slave labor. Successful warriors furnished captive women to their wives for helpers. These captive women were given the opportunity to trade their slave status for wifehood, and captive girls were carefully trained to become Comanche wives. Captive boys were trained as warriors to fill the vacancies in the warrior ranks. In addition to members of other tribes, Anglos, Spaniards, and Mexicans were abducted to be made slaves.

In Comanche society, once a woman left her father's camp she must of necessity become a wife. There was not another nook or cranny of Comanche society into which she could crowd herself. There were no avocations open to her. Prostitution and concubinage were not countenanced, and the enslavement of an unattached Comanche woman by another Comanche was completely unthinkable. (An example of the length to which a Comanche's obligation to respect the rights of other Comanches extended may be seen in the situation of the semiwild dogs that infested every camp. These dogs were not pets—they were parasites. But they could be neither killed nor mistreated. They were relatives of the coyote; and since the coyote was a relative of the Comanche, one had as well abuse another Comanche as one of these semiwild dogs.)

Provision for widows was made in this manner: if a man was killed, or if he died from disease, his wives became the wives of his brother or brothers, and his children became the children of his brother or brothers. There was also a relationship known as blood brotherhood, in which two men mingled their blood together. Such a blood brother could succeed as the husband of his deceased blood brother's wives.

During the more than five years when I was among the Comanches and was dealing with them, I became sold on polygamy as a way of life for them. They made it work. After twenty-six years of peace, there continued to be a much larger number of women than men. Though all but three of the old warrior group that I knew had more than one wife, and a number had three or more, I knew of no single man in that age group. Neither were there surplus unattached women. And women must have outnumbered men in the age group of forty-five years and over, by considerably more than two to one.

As nearly as I was able to discover, the multiple wife situation was a development rather than the result of a plan. A man did not decide he was going to have two, three, or more wives and go out and purchase the number he had decided upon. He started modestly, as a young warrior, with the purchase of one wife. Then as he prospered, gained a reputation, and accumulated a horse herd and maybe a baby or two, the work would become too heavy for one wife. Obviously they couldn't secure a hired girl, so they looked around and probably decided between them who would make a satisfactory and agreeable number two wife. When possible, a younger sister of the number one wife was purchased. Sisters often trained themselves so that they could be wives of the same man, one learning to be a good horse-woman and the other to be expert in the tanning of hides and making of clothes, one complementing the other, in the hope that they might be purchased at the same time and so remain together.

If, in due time, there came to be need of a third wife, the rule was that she be young and healthy, capable of taking over the burdens of the older women. When the young wife bore a baby for the camp there was rejoicing, not only by the husband but by the other wives as well. This was especially true if it was a boy baby. (This part appealed to me. Just think of a family life where they never ran out of babies!)

I never once saw an older wife scold or mistreat the child of another wife. In fact, I never saw a Comanche woman mistreat any woman's child. It was no uncommon sight to see one wife caring for the children, while the other wife or wives were working, say, at hauling up wood for the camp.

At the time when I knew them, the Comanches were still living strictly a camp life. Where it was possible, the Indian Department had fenced the family allotments all into one enclosure or pasture, using four strands of barbed wire and posts every rod. The department had also built each family a box house—in most instances measuring four-teen by twenty-eight feet, shingle-roofed, and set on a foundation of rock piers about four feet apart.

Obviously, a family consisting of the husband, two to three wives, and several children could not live in a space that small. For spring, summer, and fall use a family would construct a brush arbor. Forked posts were cut so as to be about seven or eight feet tall when the lower end was set in the ground. Poles were laid from one fork to another, and in turn numerous cross poles were laid on them. Then a thick layer of brush with leaves was piled on the cross poles. This layer was thick enough to repel the sun's heat and shed the water from a rea-sonable rain. From time to time, as they were needed, additional lay-ers of brush were applied.

This arbor served as living quarters for the family the greater part of the year. Since the sides were left open, whatever breeze there was, from whichever direction it came, was utilized. Platforms, placed on forked sticks and about three feet from the ground, served as beds.

The cooking was done on an open fire, just below the bank of a slough and at some distance from the arbor. Brooms made from the native broom weeds tied tightly to a stick handle, brush end down, were used to sweep the arbor and cooking area scrupulously clean; and there were surprisingly few flies around the arbor. Generally shade was available, and the eating was done under the trees, away from the arbor. Wood, of course, was the fuel for the campfire.

When the time came for the really bad weather of fall, tents were pitched. Some families still had tepee poles and canvas covering for them. The buffalo-hide coverings had been gone for a long time when I arrived on the scene. The tents and tepees, together with the house, supplied the shelter needed in truly bad weather.

I have been in and around camps many times, and on occasion have even found it necessary to stay for the night. I watched the division of labor, seeking to find a clue as to who bossed whom. I never arrived at any satisfactory answers. Apparently the husband kept hands off, and the cooking area may have been out of bounds for him. At least, he stayed clear until the call for food. I never saw any of the women seek advice from the husband while the preparation of the meal was in progress.

There were exceptions, but at the home camp the husband usually corralled the horses and roped the ones to be used. Generally one of the women would come and help him harness or saddle up. Apparently the same wife helped with the horses each time. I was never aware of an order being given. When a family was in camp on the reservation for its Grass Money, the husband ordinarily cared for the horses.

At the home camp, one or two of the squaws would take a team and the wagon into the woods for the camp's wood supply. The squaws selected the down timber and chopped it into small enough pieces so that they could load it on the wagon to be hauled to camp. In one family group, this task was permanently assigned to a wife who had been so indiscreet as to give birth to a white baby. (The displeasure was not, however, visited upon the child. Not only was it treated just the same as the other children, but at times I was inclined to think it was actually the husband's favorite.)

I never saw anything to indicate that the first or oldest wife was necessarily the favorite one, nor was I able to tell which one of the women established the division of labor. A more trained observer than I might have secured more accurate information. In any event, of these things I am sure: there was a division of labor, and each wife went about her tasks cheerfully and willingly. Whichever one of the women divided the labor reserved enough for herself so that she was just as busy as the other women.

The little girls of the family stayed close to the women the day through, and performed tasks suitable for their ages. But the little boys roamed far and wide, never seeming to have any duties except when they were helping their father with the horses.

During group tasks there was always quite a bit of conversation and considerable laughing. In warm weather the women would go to the creek together, select a place in the shade where the water was about six or eight inches deep, and sit in the water on the sandy bottom to do the family wash. I never learned what the talk and laughter were about, as I was never able to accumulate a squaw vocabulary. (Comanche women held only the most necessary conversation with any man, Indian or white, other than their own menfolks. And while I was generally able to figure out the subject of the men's conversation and follow its progress, I seldom recognized a word used by the women when they conversed among themselves. At times I was inclined to think they even had a different language.)

The same air of camaraderie seemed to prevail whenever the wives were together in a group. I noticed it in the store whenever there was only one family present. Their trading done, the wives would draw their chairs into a group and converse. They never had chairs in their camps, but the women never passed up the several chairs we had in the store—although once in a while some quite old squaw would insist on sitting on the floor. If the chairs were all occupied, the women never hesitated to sit on the floor, and the people trading would walk around them.

Wherever you saw a man's wives—in town, on the reservation, or at a celebration—they always formed a group. You would not find one wife in a store and another out on the street. Two or more groups of wives would often chat together in the store or sit together in the shade on the reservation or at a powwow.

One custom which seemed odd to me was that of each wife's having her own sewing machine. The sewing done by the average family was not so extensive that one machine would not easily have sufficed. Yet each wife would have her own—something I had been alerted to look for by an article that had appeared in the *Star* commenting that each of Quanah Parker's wives had her individual sewing machine.

When our store opened for business, we had everything to learn about merchandising, and so we had no customs or inhibitions to overcome. I believe this operated to our advantage, especially with the Indian business. Mother selected our dry goods, and her good taste resulted in our having an attractive array of bolts of calico and gingham. Having observed the Indian women's taste in colors and the way they trimmed their clothes, she bought boxes and boxes of braid to match the colors of the piece goods. This unusual display of dry goods undoubtedly did much to attract the Indian women to our store from the very start.

I soon learned the Comanche words and phrases I needed to wait on them. I had no dictionary—as far as I know, the Comanche words had never been listed and defined. My learning was pretty much catch-as-catch-can. I found I could go a long way with the expression *Osh-a-him*. This can be translated as "What is the Comanche word for this?" or "What is this?" or "Who is that man?" or "Whose horse is this?" or "What is that man's name?" and so on and on and on, by inflection of the voice, pointing, and the use of signs.

Boylike, I was much amused at the women's way of shopping. When a family came into the store to trade, one wife would come to the grocery counter and start buying. She knew exactly what she wanted and the amount she wanted. No matter if she had been to Carlisle, if she wanted fifty cents' worth of sugar she said, "*Pina—* four bits." When I had weighed out the sugar, she paid for it and then asked for the next article, always by its Indian name and in amounts divisible by a bit, or 12½ cents. Money to the Comanches was two bits, four bits, six bits, dollar, dollar two bits, etc. Buying in this fashion would continue until all the first wife's wants were satisfied. Then she would place her purchases in a clean flour sack she had brought along for the purpose, and would rejoin the wife group.

Now a second wife would come to the counter, and in the majority of cases would buy exactly what the first wife had bought—and in identical amounts. Then it was wife number three's turn. The only variation would come when they bought the sweets for the children. Each wife bought for her own children, generally some variety of cookies that we kept on display, under glass to protect them from dirt and flies. Usually the older children had their own money and made their own purchases.

When their money ran out before payment time, we would credit those who were not heavy drinkers until the next Grass Money time. Though all merchandise was charged to the husband, the wives bought in the same way. We followed the custom of keeping the sales slip for each wife's purchases with her name, but we were never called upon to show who bought what. I wondered whether the wives had an after-payment settlement.

The women always had a lot of fun buying dry goods. We kept yardsticks laid out along the dry-goods counter so that a woman could point to the particular bolt she was interested in. Each bought for herself and her children; but as each made her choices, the other wife or wives stood by the counter and passed remarks freely about her selections. These remarks always caused much merriment, not only within the group itself but also from other Indian women listening in.

One white custom at which the Comanche women never ceased to wonder was the freedom with which white women would converse with men other than those of their own families. A homesteader's wife who had not talked to anyone but her husband for two weeks would come in plumb full of talk. As she was doing her buying, she would tell me all about the crops, the new calves or colts, and where she and her husband would be driving to church or a picnic the next day. In turn she would want to know all about what happened in town, who had had a baby, who had died, and all the gossip. Meanwhile Indian women who had, I knew, been to Carlisle or Chilocco would be listening very intently and talking in low tones to other women sitting near, apparently describing the conversation.

Comanche men and boys could scarcely help being vain, with all the attention the women and girls of the family bestowed upon them. This was especially apparent when the family as a whole was going to a gathering of any kind, white or Indian. The women would have the finest of shirts and neck scarves prepared for the husband and the boys to wear for the occasion. Often the shirt and bandana would be made from the finest red or pink silk. Nearly all the men wore their hair long, and the husband would sport a new hairdo with strips of otter skin or fancy yarn braided in with the hair to increase the size of the braid. The white sheet that was rolled up and worn around the waist like a sash had been washed and sun-bleached until it was of a dazzling whiteness.

The women and girls rode in the wagon or hack, but the men and boys would be mounted on their finest horses. Their saddles and bridles would be polished, and each would be carrying a gaudy quirt. I got the impression that when the men and boys were put on parade like this, they belonged to the whole family of women and girls. At least, they would all be equally puffed up with pride; It wouldn't have done to have pricked any one of them with a needle.

I grew up in a society where we all had Sunday clothes put away for special occasions. But this Comanche custom of dolling up the men and boys carried a greater significance for them. It was of a ritualistic nature.

To sum up: contrary to the impression of inner family turmoil I had received from the accounts in the *Star* and the *Journal* of the workings of polygamy, the Comanche made it work. As far as the older Comanches were concerned, it had been and was an ideal arrangement.

To all appearances, everyone involved in the multiple wife setup— the husband, the wives, the children—was quite happy with it. I never observed a quarrel between wives. I never saw one wife mistreat another. Nor did I ever observe a display of jealousy in relation to either husband or child.

MY FRIEND CHARLEY ROSS

IT MUST HAVE BEEN close to the first of December, 1902, when early one morning the second norther of a mild fall struck. Like the first one, it wasn't a true blue norther, and during the day several light showers came over, hitching rides on the hurrying wind.

Soon the small amount of moisture from each shower was worked into the dirt of our street, without ever having had a chance to run off. By night the street was well cut up. Then the real cold arrived. By morning our street was frozen solid in its chopped-up condition. When the sun came up, it found the clouds cleared away; but the wind was as vicious and stinging as it had been the day and night before. Dad had mail he wanted to leave on the morning mail hack, so I put on about all the clothes I owned and started for the post office.

Our main business street in the little town of Faxon, Indian Territory, was only two blocks long, and most of the buildings, including ours, were on the north side. There were only scattered buildings on the south side of the street. All the buildings were one story, except the one where the post office was located. It was a story and a half, and the merchant-postmaster and his family lived upstairs. Dad's building, of box type construction, had a frame false front which extended full width as high as the comb of the roof.

As I stepped out of the store door, two little Indian wagons, without bows or canvas and with only one outrider, turned into the street from the southeast trail. With the pony teams at a brisk trot the miniature lumber wagons rattled and bumped toward me over the rough frozen ground.

Ours was the farthest store west, with only a wagon yard beyond. Deciding that the wagons were heading for our store, I waited to see who was in them. Looking into the early morning as I was, I couldn't tell. When they were about a half-block away they came out of the sun's rays, and I saw it was the Charley Ross family and the family of his brother-in-law To-pet-chy, with Charley Ross riding horseback. Then the women and children in the wagons began smiling and shouting, "*Hi-hites Para-da-de-a! Hi-hites Para-da-de-a!*" They were looking right at me.

The Comanche country had been our home—Dad's, Mother's, and mine—for about seven months. I had been trying desperately to learn a Comanche vocabulary sufficient for use in the store Dad had started, and as much as possible about the different Indian families living in our trade territory. Both of these families had been trading at the store. Charley Ross seemed to be one of the very few educated Indians who would talk readily with white people. He was several years older than the other Indians who had been away to school.

The women drivers turned their pony teams in to our hitchrack; but instead of getting out, they sat there smiling and shouting, along with the children, "*Hi-hites Para-da-de-a!*" Charley swung down from his saddle, left his horse ground hitched, and, smiling, came up to me and put a hand on either shoulder. "Know what the women and children are saying?" he asked.

I shook my head. "I know *hi-hites*. It's a sort of hello, but a hello you only say to a friend."

"They are saying your new name. Your Comanche name. *Para-da-de-a*. Means Big Boy."

This sudden honor—I realized it was an honor—left me tongue-tied with embarrassment. Charley saved the day for me by continuing, "The Comanches like the way you treat them when they come into the store. They like the way you live. They want you to have a Comanche name. Then other Indians, Indians who don't know you, will know you are to be trusted, because your Comanche friends give you a Comanche name."

This is how it happened that Charley Ross became my friend, instead of just another Indian customer of the store. He was to live thirty-eight more years, and the friendship beginning that day continued to the end. Often there was a stretch of years between our meetings, but when we did meet we made up for lost time. And over the years I came to know him as the man who, I believe, did more to bring about an amicable relationship between our two races than any other man, Indian or white.

The Comanche Agency roll gives Che-appy (pronounced Ce-Pa, with a soft C and the accent on the first syllable), the Indian name under which Charley Ross was listed, the birth year of 1863. This means that in 1875, when the roll was compiled, a government clerk considered that he appeared to be twelve years old. His father's name is given as To-wa, and his mother's as Wer-e-kah. No birth years are given for either the father or the mother, nor is there any record of their death. But four or five years later Che-appy is listed as an orphan, and he may well have been an orphan at the time of his enrollment. This means that his father left no surviving brother or blood brother. Had there been such an uncle, Che-appy would have become his son, and thus not an orphan. As to the manner of the father's death, we know only that Charley Ross's daughter Ida (now Mrs. Phil Cato of Riverside, California) is sure that her grandfather was not killed while fighting.

Che-appy was born during the last years of the Comanche empire, Comanchería, which stretched from the Arkansas River to the north and the Cross Timbers to the east to the varying southern and western boundaries formed by the range of the southern herd of buffalo, whose guardians the Comanches considered themselves to be. Nothing is definitely known of his early childhood, but it is probable that he was held prisoner, as were most Comanche women and children, during the all-out effort of the Army to subdue the Comanches following the battle of Adobe Walls and until the final surrender in 1875. While this relentless warfare was being waged against the Comanche, on an around-the-clock basis, twelve months of the year, with at times as many as five columns of troops in the field, every horse and mule belonging to the Indians was shot and killed as soon as it was captured, to prevent its recapture. Following the engagement at Palo Duro Canyon, the Army slaughtered 1,400 head of Comanche horses and mules. Then, when the Army wanted to move the captured women and children to the reservation, it had no transportation for them. Everyone who was able was required to walk. An old friend of mine, Wer-que-yah, if he was in the mood and was properly urged, would relate how he, along with many others, including Peet-so, the girl he later married, walked several hundred miles to Fort Sill, in the winter. While this was going on, the hide hunters, with the Army's blessing, were destroying the remnant of the buffalo.

This was Che-appy's childhood background. The first that is definitely known about him, after his appearance on the tribal roll, concerns his presence at the Carlisle Indian School in Pennsylvania, which was established in 1879 by General (then Captain) Richard H. Pratt. Norman G. Holmes, area tribal relations officer of the Anadarko Agency, has found letters and copies of letters that passed between Superintendent Pratt and others at Carlisle and the Indian agent at Fort Sill, whose name was Hunt. One letter to Hunt, dated April 18, 1883, signed by H. Price, states that during the following summer certain pupils, among whom was "Cheapie Ross," would complete the three-year period for which they had been sent to Carlisle. This would mean that Charley Ross began his schooling in the fall of 1880, the beginning of the second year of the school's existence.

The majority of the children in the first student body had been Northern Sioux. Washington officials insisted that Pratt take part of his students from this source, so that they would be hostages against another outbreak of the Sioux. He personally secured 84 Sioux children. He then sent three emissaries into the Southwest, and also wrote to various agents there. This effort netted him 52 more students, bringing the total to 136—16 more than had been authorized by the order establishing the school.

For some time I wondered why other Comanches in our trade territory who were about the same age as Charley could not speak English and had not been to school. Among them was Charley's brother-in-law To-pet-chy, Yok-so-wy, Coffee, and Wer-que-yah, of whom I have spoken. The next oldest Indian I knew who spoke English was Andrew Per-da-sof-pa, who was about ten years younger. His sister and a brother also went to Carlisle. One reason for the gap is, I believe, that when Carlisle was first opened it was too soon after the surrender for teen-age Comanche children to trust themselves to a school run by the white man's army, and especially by one of the officers who had been leading the fight against them. Then too, General Pratt took only fifty-two students from the Southwest area in

1879 and fifty-nine in 1889. This area included the Cheyenne-Arapaho Agency and the Pawnee Agency, as well as the Agency at Fort
Sill. Agent Hunt had the Comanches, Apaches, Caddo, Wichita, Kee-
ichi, and Kiowa under his supervision, and so no one tribe could have
sent many students.

As for Che-appy, his daughter recalls his saying that because he
was an orphan and had no one to look after him, he was picked up
and sent when pupils were being sought. Human nature seems much
the same everywhere: here was a chance to rid the tribe of an orphan.

The letters found by Mr. Holmes indicate that Che-appy was
given an Anglo surname at the school, as became the custom. The
children's Indian names were too much for the teachers. One letter
from General Pratt to Agent Hunt, dated August 27, 1881, listed
certain students from Hunt's Agency who were in school, and in the
list was "Cheapie Ross." Another, dated August 6, 1882, states that
"Cheapie Ross," among others, "is here and quite well." The letter
also states that "Cheapie" was out for a while during harvest, and was
praised for his excellent work. It was a custom of the school to place
students, both boys and girls, out to work for the nearby German
farmers during the summer vacation. These summer jobs were called
"outings." Another of Charley's summer outings, according to his
daughter, was in the John Wanamaker store in New York City,
where he worked as a stockboy.

A copy of one letter sent to General Pratt, dated June 15, 1882,
states that Joshua Givens, having neither father nor mother, should be
allowed to decide for himself whether he would remain in school. It
may be assumed that Che-appy, since he was also an orphan, had the
same privilege when his three years came to an end. I do not know
how long he remained in school, if he did decide to stay longer than
the initial three-year period. The next Agency record of him is the
date of his marriage to Tits-se-na, also called Nah-vo-ne-vi-chy, by
Indian custom. This was in 1889. The marriage was ended forty-five
years later by the death of Tits-se-na. Four daughters and a son were
born to this union. Though polygamy was the practice of the Comanches at the time, Charley took but one wife.

Mrs. Ross never had the privilege of schooling, but she evidently
did yeoman service in the rearing of the family. She was a quiet-
mannered person, but her smile was as contagious as was her husband's. Also, I distinctly remember how easily their two little girls

smiled. Even Charley's old father-in-law, Mi-he-suah, a veteran of many years on the People's war trails and one of the first casualities of the battle of Adobe Walls, let his face light up now and then with a happy smile; and Mrs. To-pet-chy, the sister-in-law, and her children smiled often. Smiling Comanches were rare, and when one saw a smile on the face of one of the old fellows, it seemed a bit of a miracle.

Charley's first job in Oklahoma was with the Chilocco Indian School. Next he worked for the Kiowa Agency at Anadarko. Then came the opportunity to work for Sam Burnett as a cowboy on the Burnett Ranch in Texas. Charley and Sam Burnett became good friends—the Burnetts, father and son, had the reputation of getting on well with the Indians—and while Charley worked on the ranch he also became acquainted with many other Texas cattlemen. Mrs. Cato especially remembers his having spoken of the Waggoners.

The Burnett Ranch occupied much of the land between Wichita Falls and the Red River to the north. Sam Burnett also rented grass from Quanah Parker on the north side of the river, and he was one of the Texas cattlemen and grass users who in 1884 built a house for Quanah on the bank of West Cache Creek, northwest of the present town of Cache, Oklahoma. When the Indian Department took over the leasing of the grass, Burnett continued his leasing until the country was opened for homesteading.

From Albert Clark, a half-blood Comanche employed at the Ana-darko Agency, I learned that Charley Ross acquired his Anglo first name while he worked for Sam Burnett. Mr. Clark's parents had moved to the present town of Faxon, where they lived close to Char-ley, and as a lad Mr. Clark often talked to him. On one occasion Charley told young Albert the story of his name. One night, he said, the cowhands were all sitting around the wagon eating, when Sam Burnett called Che-appy to come and sit by him. He told Che-appy that he didn't like his name and was going to give him a better one. "From now on," he said, "your name is Charley Ross."

When I learned that Charley had worked as a cowboy for Sam Burnett, I understood something about him that had bothered me. I remembered Charley as a very graceful horseman, like all the Co-manches, who sat their horses as if they belonged there and nowhere else. Charley had an extra grace, especially in his mounting and dis-mounting, which were done with an even flow of only the necessary movements. Perhaps the proper word is rhythm. But my mental picture of him always had him mounting his horse from the left side, white-man fashion; and his daughter, Mrs. Cato, says that my memory is correct. The Spaniards had been the Comanches' riding teachers, and because in Spain a horse is mounted from the right side, the Comanches mounted from the right. Charley Ross, however, learned from the Burnett cowboys to mount from the left. From them he also must have learned to train his saddle horse to the ground hitch, in which the rider drops his reins to the ground and the horse stands until the reins are picked up again. As far as I know, this is a cowboy trick.

Certain of Charley's physical characteristics, though they were especially evident when he was swinging on or off his horse, came not from his days on the Burnett ranch, but from his earlier years at Carlisle. A distinguishing feature of the Carlisle Indians, which Charley possessed, was their straight, long legs, which contrasted with the bandy legs of the warrior group. The old fellows showed the effect of a lifetime spent horseback. Also, Charley was typical of the products of the Indian boarding schools in being some inches taller than most of the Comanches of his generation or older, who ranged in height from five feet four inches to five feet six. Charley was five feet ten or eleven inches tall. The balanced diet the students at the schools received, the regular meals, the protection from the elements, and the smaller amount of horseback riding during the growing years probably account for the extra height of both boys and girls and the loss of the bandy look from their legs.

Though Charley was like the rest of the returning Carlisle students in these bodily ways, he was very different from them in his attitudes. It was as though the others shed the school years, and everything connected with them, and shoved it all under a log on West Cache. When they came into our store to make a purchase, they asked for it by its Indian name. They never uttered a word of English if grunting or pointing would get the job done. Nor would they interpret for us, even when it would be to the advantage of an older Indian. For example, one of the older Indians might have a check he had received for the sale of a horse or steer, but he would know nothing but what he had been told concerning its amount. We would be willing to cash the check, but we needed to know that the Indian was aware of the sum named in it. There might be a number of educated young Indians around, but it would be almost impossible to find one who would explain to the older man the amount of the check and look to see that we gave him the right amount of money.

In contrast, Charley was always ready to ease the contact between the two races. He sought and found many ways to aid his people in their dealings with the white settlers. Among the tasks which he allotted to himself was that of translating for ministers. Much of the effort to bring the Christian religion to the Comanche was made by ministers unfamiliar with the language. I knew only two ministers who could exhort in the Comanche tongue. The rest had to depend on interpreters when they were preaching. According to Mrs. Cato, her father and mother were charter members of the Baptist church organized at the Deyo Mission on Blue Beaver Creek, west of Lawton and south of the Wichitas. Charley Ross became interpreter for various missionaries connected with the Northern Baptist Convention, now known as the American Baptist Convention. His children and grandchildren are helping to carry on the work of this church organization. Following the death of Reverend Deyo's wife, his brother-in-law, a Mr. Given, and his wife lived at the Deyo Mission parsonage and helped Mr. Deyo carry on his work. When Charley's son was born he was named Given, in honor of this good man. That son, Given M. Ross, now lives in Oklahoma City.

Charley also acted as interpreter in government matters. Of course, I was never present when conferences were held between government officials and tribal leaders, but I am sure Charley was often there as interpreter. I have seen him both in state courts and in the United States District Court, acting as the official interpreter in order that an Indian might have his day in court. On at least one occasion he was used as an interpreter before a legislative committee at the state capitol. This, I believe, was during the consideration of a bill to abolish the Peyote Religious Ceremony. Charley was one who made the wishes of the old fellows known to the state legislature.

These are some of the ways in which Charley Ross spent his long and busy life, smoothing the path between the two races. His task was not easy. Hostility, animosity, bigotry, avarice, and suspicion, if not openly apparent, were but thinly camouflaged on either side when the white man and the Indian were at odds.

In such situations, an interpreter must have the confidence of both parties, or confusion results. One example concerns the signing, in October, 1892, at Fort Sill, of the Jerome Agreement, between the government and the several interested tribes, which finally resulted in the opening of the Comanche, Kiowa, and Caddo reservations to white homesteading. Many Indian leaders protested the agreement after their own interpreters had explained it to them. They maintained that Joshua Given (the same one mentioned in one of the letters to General Pratt at Carlisle), who was the son of the deceased Kiowa Chief Satank, had translated their demands to the commission inaccurately and had falsely represented what the written agreement contained.

In great rage, the Indian leaders made medicine to bring about Joshua Given's death, as well as the demise of the commissioners. Making an image to represent Given, they threw mud at it. The fatal seizure would take hold where the mud hit the image. The mud struck the image in the chest. On his way home from the council, Joshua Given was stricken by a hemorrhage from the lungs, and shortly thereafter he died.

When old Indians told this story, they had the members of the commission following the young Kiowa in death. At any rate, history bears the old ones out as to the untimely death of Joshua Given.

Some of the Indian leaders decided to take their grievance to their Great White Father in Washington. Choosing their own interpreter this time, they told their story to Grover Cleveland. President Cleveland assured them that their land would not be taken from them during his administration. Their trip delayed the opening of their land for homesteads for nine years. But in 1901 the Jerome Agreement was implemented. Each Indian then living was allowed an allotment of 160 acres. This represented the Indian's individual share of the once great empire, Comanchería. The white man got the rest.

When they had had such experiences, the older Indians were bound to have certain suspicions of Charley Ross, with his numerous white man's ways, white man's language, and friendships with white men. But he was devoted to the old fellows and had their respect. One symbol of the links he kept with them was the braids he wore, even though he wore a hat and his hair was scanty. I remember having thought of the braids as affected. But finally age and observation taught me better. The older Indians all wore their hair in braids, and these were the people he must stay close to so that he could help them.

He had other bonds with the old fellows besides his braids. He had a wife who spoke no English. He was fulfilling a Comanche tradition by caring for his wife's parents. Mrs. Ross's father, Mi-he-suah, lived in Charley's home, though his son To-pet-chy's home was only a short distance away, on the east side of West Cache Creek. And though a Jesus Man (Christian), he belonged to a native Baptist church.

I am sure I felt a bit of intellectual awe in the presence of Charley Ross, and this was renewed at our meetings over the years. Here was a man, it must be remembered, who was born into a stone-age culture that was without knowledge of the smelting of iron or any other metal, and without the skill to forge tools from metal already smelted. From the viewpoint of the white people of that time, the Comanches were murderers, rapists, home-burners, kidnappers of women and children, horse thieves, cattle thieves, and all-round savages. History justifies this opinion, but there is this saving grace for the Comanche: he was here first. The white man was the invader. The empire of Comanchería had been forged and was in existence more than eighty-five years before George Washington became president of the United States. From the ruins of this empire came Charley Ross, who first found a way to enter the white man's world and then set about softening the impact between the two races that events decreed should live side by side. Mrs. Cato wrote in a letter to me, "My father was a very intelligent man, above the average, and so very much interested in higher education for his race of people and his own children. Even though he himself did not receive full benefit of complete education, he had the mind of a college graduate."

What a man accomplishes during his lifetime does not complete his true measurement. One must also judge how well he has projected himself into the next generation by adding the accomplishments of his children. Charley Ross's son-in-law, Mr. Cato, has told me that at the end of the 1965-66 school year Charley's children and grandchildren had completed forty-seven years of teaching. Others, not teachers, hold responsible positions with railroads, oil companies, and hospitals.

I have emphasized Charley Ross's pleasant manners and ready smile. But there was no servility about him, nor did he ever attempt to please everyone at the cost of any sacrifice of principle. He was a positive character about whom I never heard a derogatory word, either from whites, many of whom were always looking for a flaw or chink in his armor of friendliness, or from his tribesmen, who tended to distrust any Indian who earned the friendship of white people. He went about his self-appointed task of being a catalyst for the two races with good will and common sense.

FOUR QUANAH PARKER STORIES

~~~~~~

QUANAH PARKER WANTED TO BUY A STOVE

THE UNSEASONABLE NORTHER caught us unawares. In the Southwest country you never realize it is the fall of the year. The hot days that are August trail on over into September, and then they gentle off into pleasantly warm ones. You realize that the long days have lent some time to the nights and made them just right for sleeping, but it is still "fishin' and swimmin'" weather to the hardier souls.

When we had gone to bed the night before, there had been no indications that morning would find this blast from the Arctic venting its spleen on our pleasant prairie countryside. As it slashed southward, one splattering shower chased another closely, but not closely enough to be a continuous rain. They were more like a whole series of furies out for a romp.

We had planned for winter enough to bring the heating stove from the claim and set it up in the store. By the time I got the mules in their shelter Dad had a good fire going, and Mother was fixing a warm breakfast on her little gasoline stove. Breakfast over, there was little else to do but enjoy the heat from the stove. Since we got to town we had not seen another soul hardy enough to be out of doors. Just as we had had no warning of the Arctic onslaught, even so we had no forewarning that this was to be the busiest day of the store's history.

About the time we were wondering what we would do with ourselves during the long day in front of us, the Indians began to arrive in their little canvas-covered wagons.

The first two or three dozen wagons used up all the hitchracks in the little town. By noon there must have been 150 of the little miniature prairie schooners parked around the group of buildings that was our town. When the hitchracks were filled, the later arrivals pulled up out on the grass, unhitched, and tied the horses to the rear wheels of the wagons.

These were not our Indians. These were Comanches from the west and north, along the south side of the Wichita Mountains. All of them were in at least the second day of their journey. They were on their way to an ancient tribal gathering place, across the Red River in Texas. Bands of Comanches had been using this gathering place since before there were white men in North Texas.

Apparently they had arranged to rendezvous at our little settlement, the last trading place on their trail, and make the rest of their journey together. In a little over two miles they would enter the Pasture Reserve, and it would be two more days' journey to the river. The ancient gathering place was on land controlled by the Burnett Ranch. The Burnetts, who had a history of getting along with the Comanches, encouraged the Indians to continue gathering there for their tribal powwows.

Just as there had been a shortage of hitchracks, soon there was a shortage of floor space in the store. For hours the only unoccupied floor was behind the counters. Of course the focal point for everyone—men, squaws, and children—was the stove. After slightly more than sixty years, I still have no desire to describe the scent of all those damp bodies crowded together, mingled with the steam rising from the clothing of those fortunate enough to get within the radius of the stove's heat.

I never knew when our Indians, that is to say the Indians living in our trade territory, joined these strange Comanches. They may even have started the day before. During the several hours these Indians were in town, I saw but an occasional face I had seen before. They were laying in a food supply to last during the time of their gathering, and as a result, by the time we had their wants appeased, our staple groceries were exhausted.

Owing to the inclement weather, they likewise stripped us of bedding, underwear, socks and stockings, etc. If there had been six more clerks, we could have used them all. Somewhere near the middle of this selling-buying nightmare, I was aware of a large, tall Indian crowding in front of the Indian I was waiting on. He was taller than anyone else in the store, including myself, though I was approaching six feet. With his large black Stetson hat, well-fitted blue serge suit, blue flannel shirt, and obviously bench-made, high-heeled cowboy boots, he was dressed like a prosperous cattleman.

His copper color and the large braid hanging down on either side of his face onto his chest proclaimed him an Indian—not only an Indian, but obviously one of the Old Fellows. This was my private designation of the Indians old enough to have ridden the war trails. They had to be in their very late forties and upward. None of this group had been to school, nor would they have spoken English if they had known how.

This well-dressed Indian now surprised me by asking in perfect English, "How much do you want for that stove?"

This was the first time we had had a fire in the stove; but the fact that it was the only heating stove we had, plus the dozens of people—men, squaws, children—who had been crowding around it for hours, and were still crowding around it, and then the fact that I was just entered into my fifteenth year, all combined to hit my funny bone. I laughed as I answered him, "It couldn't be worth much of anything. It is just an old stove that came with our claim. But it is the only stove we have to keep the storeroom warm. We couldn't sell it."

With an air I am sure he considered superior, but which bordered more on the arrogant, the way he had been arrogant in crowding in front of the Indian I had been waiting on instead of awaiting his turn, he thrust his hand into his trousers pocket, brought out a wad of bills, and began looking through them.

As he was running through the bills, he continued talking: "You have this good house to live in. My women and children will live in a tent now. They need this stove. You don't. Here, I'll give you $20 for the stove." And he waved a twenty-dollar gold certificate at me.

Realizing how much in earnest this Indian was about the stove, I shook my head, saying, "The stove is not worth anywhere near such a sum. But we need it ourselves. We have a hardware store here now. Have you tried there?"

He continued to wave the bill at me as he answered, "Of course. I went there the first thing, when I got to town."

I needed to get rid of this Indian and get back to those that were buying supplies. Only when I had all their wants satisfied would I be able to feed my stomach, which was complaining at the way it was being treated. I tried another way to get rid of him by saying, "The stove is not mine to sell or not sell. It belongs to my father. He is up front on the dry goods side. The bald-headed man. Go talk to him."

Tall as I was, I could watch him make his way to where Dad was selling cotton hose to some young Indian women. I could see he was using the same arrogant tactics he had used on me. He pushed himself in front of the women, holding the bill level with Dad's face. From the quizzical look Dad was wearing, it was taking him a while to realize the drift of what the tall Indian had in mind. When he understood, he frowned, shook his head, and turned back to his stocking customers.

The Indian made his way to the door and left the store.

Searching for a familiar face, I spied the auburn Vandyke of the little preacher from the Dea Mission on Blue Beaver, back to the north and east. He was standing a few bodies away from me. When I was able to make my way to him I asked, "Who was that tall well-dressed Indian that was trying to buy our stove?"

I never knew whether it was disappointment, dismay, or awe as he answered with both caps and quotes in his voice, "You don't know? That was Quanah Parker, the great War Chief of the Comanches."

It took the passage of several years to bring me enough maturity to realize that this was possibly the first request a white man had refused Quanah Parker in many years. It is entirely probable that as little as eighteen months previous to that time, and before this land had been opened for white settlement, had Quanah Parker asked a white trader to sell him his stove, the trader would have drawn the fire, carried the stove out-of-doors, cleaned it of ashes, loaded it on the chief's wagon, and insisted it be accepted as a gift. His goodwill had been a must for many years to anyone doing business in the Comanche area, even though it was business conducted through the Indian Department.

Somewhere around 3:00 to 3:30 P.M., the Indians began hitching up their teams, loading up their supplies and their families, and heading south. In an hour or so there was not an Indian in town. We could now draw a long breath, feed our empty stomachs, and start bringing order out of chaos. Outside the streets were as deserted as when we had driven in that morning. Our little clump of buildings, visible for many miles as they sat on a high rise of ground, continued to be buffeted by the scuds of scattering raindrops driven by the Arctic blast on its way to the southlands.

As for the stove, the old chunk-burner continued to warm the store for the several years my father continued to operate it, and it was still in place when he decided to retire and sold the business to his successor.

Nau-noc-ca's Wedding Clothes

LABOR DAY, 1918, found me in as unlikely a place to pick up a Quanah Parker story as I could imagine. I had been at Camp Hickory in Tennessee for some weeks, and this was my first opportunity to get away, even for a few hours.

The evening before, I had arranged with the cook to have me a sack lunch ready when I came for an early early breakfast. I was away on my nine-mile walk to Andrew Jackson's old home, the Hermitage, before sunup, and arrived there as the custodian and his wife were finishing their breakfast.

When they found I had walked the nine miles from Camp Hickory and expected to walk back, they treated me like royalty. I am sure they allowed me to miss little if anything—whether it was the beautiful dining room, the carriage house, the separate kitchen where the slaves had prepared the food, the rose garden, the graves, or the old slave quarters. The next visitor did not arrive until eleven o'clock, so they had plenty of time.

While I sat down by the spring, eating my noonday lunch, the custodian came down and sat with me so that he could brag a bit about the spring. I had noticed a two-inch pipe leaving the spring, and he told me it furnished the water supply for the Confederate Soldier's Home, located a mile or so down the valley, and on the west or opposite side.

When I had shown my respects to General Jackson and still had most of the afternoon left, I decided to visit the Confederate Home. In planning my approach to the old Rebels, I decided it would be best to tell them I was the son of a First Vermont Cavalryman, before trying to become too chummy.

About fifteen of the old soldiers were sitting on the east veranda or gallery of a huge, three-story, unpainted firetrap. I knew by their doleful expressions that they were all in a bad humor, and shortly I found out why. On holidays and Sundays they got only two meals. After breakfast the help would all leave, and they would return only in time to cook supper. Furthermore, the help carefully locked all kitchen and dining room doors before leaving.

I stopped at the foot of the steps leading up to the porch, and grinned as I looked from one glum face to another, but I never got the slightest ripple in return. Then I tried another tack. "As sour as you all look," I said, "I don't believe it's safe for the son of a First Vermont Cavalryman to come up on the porch for a visit."

That broke the ice, and a half-dozen of the old fellows, some charging and some hobbling, came down the steps and bade me welcome. When they found I was from Oklahoma, the full thaw set in. Nearly all of them had relatives: a son, daughter, niece, some kin they wanted to tell me about, that had gone to Oklahoma. My law practice had taken me to practically every county in the state, and I was familiar with nearly every town they mentioned. I could tell them a little about the town and the surrounding country.

One old chap had never moved or said a word. He was an Indian. His broad frame indicated that he had been a powerful man in his time. His high-heeled boots, the worse for wear, were hooked over the lower round of a straight-backed, cane-bottomed chair. The chair was propped back against the side of the building, and he had pulled his large gray hat down over his eyes until it rested on his nose. His long arms were folded across his chest.

The rest of the old fellows had been visiting with me for perhaps an hour, when the Indian, without moving his body or lifting his hat, spoke. "Did you ever know anyone in Oklahoma by the name of Emmet Cox?" he asked.

"Yes sir," I replied promptly. "I know two men by the name of Emmet Cox. One is a farmer living near Faxon in southwest Oklahoma, and the other is a Comanche squaw man. He married one of Quanah—"

That was as far as I got. The Indian's chair banged down on to all four legs, he jumped up, snatched off his large hat, and slapped his leg with it. "By God, boys," he exclaimed, "he is from Oklahoma!"

Shortened down, this is the story he told us. He was a Mississippi

Choctaw and had served in a Mississippi regiment during the war.
He had married a white woman who was a good dressmaker. They
decided to see the West from a covered wagon. When they got to
North Texas, they began working at the different ranches. His wife
would do sewing for the womenfolks, and our narrator would work
as a ranch hand.

In due time, they drifted to the Comanche country and worked
for Quanah Parker. Chief Parker was running both cattle and horses
on his ranch and was in need of a rider. The cowboy's wife sewed
for the womenfolks. But Chief Parker was having trouble. A young
Texan named Emmet Cox was running some long-horned steers on
Comanche graze, and this personable young cattleman was wanting
to marry one of Quanah's daughters, named Nau-noc-ca.

Chief Parker was willing, the bridegroom was eager; it was
Nau-noc-ca who was holding up the parade. She was a new kind of
a Comanche girl to her father. He was chief of all the Comanches,
and from time to time he was called to Washington to confer with
the President of the United States; but he no longer ruled his own
household.

When he told one of his daughters to marry this white man by a
Comanche ceremony, she said no. And she kept on saying no. This
was something the chief couldn't understand—a no, coming from one
of his own womenfolks.

Nau-noc-ca had been attending the school for Indians at Carlisle,
Pennsylvania, and she was doing her own thinking and planning.
Somewhere during her schooling she made the discovery that she
was her own woman. She had no objections to the bridegroom. It is
very possible she was flattered to be the choice of this well-to-do
young white man. She had been educated in the white man's school
at Carlisle, in the white man's ways. She herself was one-quarter
white, and she was marrying a white man. Why shouldn't she be
dressed as a white bride would dress, and be married by a white
minister? These were her demands.

All the commands of her father, all the pleadings of her intended
husband and attempted persuadings by her mother, Wec-ke-ah, went
for naught. She had lost all fear of disobeying her father, and her
decision was final. A white bride's trousseau, a wedding like a white
woman's wedding with a white Christian minister, or no wedding.

Quanah and the groom surrendered. Our Indian cowboy's wife

was told to make a list of the things a white girl would require for a wedding outfit. Consulting at all times with Nau-noc-ca as to her wishes, his wife made out the list, and Quanah sent our narrator, with the money and a packhorse, to Wichita Falls for the wedding finery.

So Nau-noc-ca married her white lover, dressed in all the furbelows and adornments a white girl could have wished, and a white missionary minister performed the ceremony.

"STRANGER HE COME"

IN THE SPRING of 1922 I found it necessary to spend a weekend at Gage, a small Northwest Oklahoma town. While I was there, an old cowman told me a story about his dealings with Quanah Parker. The old chap said he was a cowboy on the first cattle drive across the Comanche land, in what is now Oklahoma, and he was trail boss on the second herd to cross Quanah Parker's domain. This would have been shortly after the surrender of the Comanches to the Army at Fort Sill in June, 1875, and before Quanah began leasing graze to Burnett and Waggoner, Texas ranchers.

An experienced drover came to the community where his father's ranch was located, wanting to make up a trail herd of stock cattle. That is to say, he wanted a herd of mostly "she stuff"—yearling heifers to old cows—bulls, and yearling steers. He proposed to drive this herd to Wyoming, where there was a market for stock cattle with Wyoming ranchers.

He had made a number of drives to Dodge City, Kansas, and had seen such herds being put together from rejects; cows heavy with calf, cows with calves at their sides, bulls, and steers and heifers too young or otherwise unsuited for the butcher or feed-lot buyers. These herds were being trailed to Wyoming.

My narrator got his job, largely because his father had been the first to sign up cattle for the proposed drive. The drover planned to cross Comanche land, because it would save at least 120 miles—60 east and 60 back west—and to overtake the herd by way of the Chisholm trail. Eight miles is a good day's drive of stock cattle, and this route would shorten the drive at least fifteen days. The drover had recently delivered a herd of steers to the Army at Fort Sill for issue to the Indians, and had met Quanah Parker.

The Chief had agreed, for so many large steers, to let him drive along the west side of Comanche land, skirt the west end of the Wichita Mountains (near where the town of Snyder, Oklahoma, is located), and on north to the Washita River and the Cheyenne-Arapaho country.

Moving a herd of stock cattle is much slower than trailing steers. Most of the cows were heavy with calf, and they began dropping their calves before the Red River was reached. This called for a calf wagon to haul the calves the first few days of their lives, until they were strong enough to keep up with the drive.

Reaching the river early one afternoon, they put the herd across and made camp on the north bank. The crossing was made just south of the present town of Davidson, Oklahoma. As usual, the cook wagon was stopped with the tongue pointed north, so if it was a cloudy morning they would know how to point the herd. The drover left at daybreak, taking my narrator with him, to find Quanah Parker.

Before leaving, he told his straw boss to drive due north until he sighted the mountains. Then he was to veer east enough to just skirt the west end of the main range. He said there was a sizable creek of clear sweet water flowing due west from the end of the range. It was about thirty to thirty-five miles to the mountains. The straw boss was to hold the herd there and await the arrival of the boss drover.

It was about sixty miles to Fort Sill from the place where they left the herd. Learning at the fort the location of Quanah's camp, they rode there and arranged with Quanah to rendezvous with the herd.

I was told what year this drive was made, but I no longer remember. Harry Drago, in his book *Great American Cattle Trails*, says a herd was put across the river at approximately the same spot in 1877. When a man by the name of Doan, an Indian trader at Fort Sill, learned of cattle being put across there and driven due north, he decided to put in a store on the south side of the river. From then till the end of the cattle drives in the middle eighties, this crossing was known as Doan's Crossing.

The Doans operated their store about seven years—perhaps until 1885. It is estimated that over the seven years several million longhorns were put across the river in the general vicinity of the store. Doan hired men to cut the coarse wild grass along the river and spread the hay on the sand to make a better crossing. As one layer was tramped into the sand, he had another layer spread. He charged twenty-five cents a head for cattle to cross his hay-paved crossing; but much of the time the river was tame, and drovers risked the danger of quicksand to save the toll.

Then too, many did not have the necessary funds. Even twenty-five cents a head for two to three thousand head of cattle ran into quite a sum of money, in a just-after-the-war economy. Doan's store was the jumping-off place; it was the last place to buy supplies until a town in Kansas could be reached; the last place mail could be received or sent; the last place owners could meet up with their herd or issue orders to their drovers.

Later, on the same night when my narrator and his boss joined the herd, they heard Quanah and his young men go into camp a short distance down the creek. At daylight they took a quarter of beef down to Quanah's camp and invited him to eat breakfast at the cook wagon.

By the time breakfast was over it began to rain, but they cut out the seventeen head of big steers promised Quanah, and the Indians started for Quanah's camp. But he left two of his young men to accompany the drive to the Washita River. They were to tell any other Indians who might try to stop the herd that it was paid through to the Washita.

Apparently it was the first time the young Indians had had all the coffee they could drink, and they rode to the chuck wagon soon after it made each stop. Food three times a day was also something new, and evidently they enjoyed the trip. When the Washita was reached, the boss got the stores out and gave each of the young braves a pair of jeans pants and a calico shirt.

Because of continuous rain, they held the cattle for three days at the camp where they met Quanah. The grass was excellent. As my narrator expressed it, "The grama-grass was belly high to a yearling," and the herd was healthy and putting on weight. The trip on to Wyoming was uneventful, and they were able to save nearly all the calves.

A ready market was found for the cattle, and at a better price than had been expected. Some of the cowboys decided to work a while for the ranchers buying the cattle, but this drive had gone so well that my narrator decided he wanted to try his hand at bossing a drive.

As soon as he was paid off, he sacked his saddle and made his way home by way of Kansas City. Part of the journey was made by stagecoach, part by passenger train, and part by mail hacks. He was home sooner than anyone else, including the boss, who was carrying the cattle owners' money. But the cowboy could tell them about what the different kinds of cattle brought.

He started right in securing commitments for a herd of stock cattle to start up the trail the next spring, as soon as graze was sufficient. With his father's backing, he had no trouble securing the required number. When he got his herd across the Red River the next spring, he too started for the Comanche chief's camp, and arranged a meeting at the same spot as before.

He said that when Quanah walked into their camp the morning of the rendezvous, he stopped where the rope corral for the horses had been the year before. The old cowman said it was the most luscious weed patch he had ever seen. He was sure every weed known to the Middle West was represented.

Silently, Quanah looked at the weeds for some time, then shook his head, saying, "White man he come. Stranger [weeds] he come. Indian he go."

Of course, the Chief was under the impression that the white man had brought the weeds to Comanche land; but actually the weeds were there all the time—scattered and stunted, choked back by the grasses, under normal conditions. But the horses, in and out of the corral during three days of rain, had completely destroyed the grama and mesquite sod, tramping it into the ground.

Weed seeds lying in the matted grasses now were in touch with the rich soil, and they grew and produced a sufficient seed crop to seed the coral ground completely this second year. Of course nothing ate the weeds, as there was an abundance of grass on every side.

Years later, in my time, this land was bought from the Indians and opened for homesteading by lottery. Weeds were not apparent, and many farmers looked forward to farming weed-free soil. But the farmer discovered the weeds were there; once the heavy sod was destroyed, they came on with a rush.

Somehow the weeds had managed a seed crop each year. Each year enough seed escaped the sharp eyes of the birds and seed-eating rodents to settle deep in the mesquite grass mat, preserve their species, and complete the cycle.

A House for Quanah Parker

IN THE LATTER PART of 1883 or early in 1884, Texas cattlemen persuaded Quanah Parker, that he should have for his family a house like the ones white men lived in. This was less than ten years after Quanah had led the remnant of a once great tribe into Fort Sill to surrender to the United States Army. It never occurred to Quanah to wonder why the cattlemen could afford to build him a home or to think that it had any connection with their renting tribal grassland from him at much less than its value.

Quanah chose a site for his house on West Cache Creek, soon after the creek left the mountains. The site is about three miles northwest of present-day Cache, Oklahoma. At the time there would not have been another structure from Fort Sill west to Texas, nor from the Wichita Mountains south to the Red River, a distance of forty miles.

The lumber for the house was hauled from Wichita Falls, Texas, an overall distance of sixty miles. The forty miles from the river to the site was mostly a beautiful level to slightly rolling prairie, except for the last seven miles. There the freighters would have touched the edge of the blackjack and post oak area. This scrub timber began where Post Oak Creek was forded.

On many occasions, when I was going to the Grass Money payments, I have used the Post Oak ford the freighters probably used. These payments were often made at the reservation located just west of the town of Cache. Post Oak and West Cache occupy the same bottom in this locality, and the freighters probably stayed to the west side of West Cache.

I have driven freight wagons loaded with lumber over these same prairies, although I was hauling from Lawton instead of to Wichita Falls. I assure you it was no job for a sissy. For the last forty miles of their journey, there would not have been so much as a culvert.

The lumber for Quanah's house, according to my figures, would have made fifteen to seventeen large loads—loads that would have required four to five yoke of oxen, or three span of mules. Assuming the lumber was hauled during the dry summer season, the prairie proper would have presented no problem, as it becomes almost as hard and unyielding as a cement roadway. But the first thirty miles of the journey offered three challenges.

The first, of course, was the Red River. If you catch it at low ebb, there is little water. Where there is water, the sand becomes boggy. The old-time cowboy expressed it this way: "It'll bog a saddle blanket." There was possibly a half-mile of dry sand where wagons would sink halfway to the hubs. Red River sand is a round, or smooth, sand formed by the disintegration of soft sedimentary rock, and under pressure it gives way and slides. When walking in it, I have sunk up to my ankles. It is similar to walking in a bin of wheat.

In contrast, the streambed of the West Cache is made up of sharp granite sand washed down from the Wichitas. When you ford the stream, you scarcely sink at all in the wet sand, and in the dry sand you sink only an inch or two.

Crossing the Red River would have necessitated doubling up, hitching the oxen of two or three wagons onto one wagon. One time we bogged our lead wagon in a wide mudhole, and it required the combined horsepower of three wagons to get each one through. I saw this river crossing in 1906, and I imagine it had changed but little, except for being a half-mile wider. As the river's old gouge or ditch filled with sediment, the river had compensated by widening its bed.

The group of wagons carrying the lumber for Quanah's house must have spent close to a week making this river crossing. All the while they were dragging the loads of lumber through the sand, they were faced with the danger that an unexpected rise might come down the river. A rise of eighteen inches would have kept them busy saving the oxen and mules hitched to the wagon that was crossing; the loaded wagon would probably have sunk out of sight into the sand.

The next challenge was a creek, whose name I can neither remember nor find on any of my maps. It is a deep-banked stream but carries little water in the summertime. I helped survey this area of the Reserve before it was opened for homesteading in 1906. I have an unpleasant memory of a half-day's work we had with pick and shovel to get our supply wagon across. This crossing, which had then obviously been used for a long time, could well have been the old Fort Sill-Wichita Falls trail crossing, traveled in the eighties. The creek, as 1 remember it, is about five miles from the river crossing. I would guess that a full day was spent by the lumber haulers in fording this deep-banked stream.

Next the freighters would have encountered a bearcat with an ugly temper, Deep Red Run. This creek is a full-grown brother to the smaller one I have just described. Each has cut a miniature Grand

Canyon into the red alluvial soil. In ages past, Deep Red carried enormous amounts of water. Its head is about thirty miles to the northwest of the crossing probably used by the freighters, and before it reaches the crossing it is joined by two substantial tributaries, Jack Creek and Horse Creek. It represents a considerable watershed.

Where the old trail crossed, the ancient streambed is probably a mile wide. It is now considered bottomland. The stream, winding around this bottom through the years, left numerous oxbow lakes as it shortened itself by cutting new channels. These lakes furnished excellent fishing for the homesteaders, as well as duck shooting in the fall and spring.

A Comanche name-giver must have named this stream, for its bed was well below the surrounding bottom and its exposed banks and the water it carried were truly red. Prior to the homestead era there was a good deal of timber on both sides of the stream and around the oxbow lakes. Three terraces had been left as this miniature canyon had been cut down, and the upper terraces had sizable trees growing on them. As the amount of water the stream carried decreased, Deep Red Run continued to gouge its way down into the soil.

At its crossing, the freighters would have had to block their wagons down the steep south bank, drag the loads through the stiff red mud of the streambed, and then pull them up the high bank on the north side. This must have been a formidable task, but it would have been of shorter duration than the Red River nightmare.

Once across, the freighters would probably have left the Fort Sill trail and headed north by slightly northwest toward their destination. The Fort Sill–Wichita Falls trail could not have been much of a roadway. It had been laid out in 1882, when the Fort Worth and Denver Railroad extended its tracks from Henrietta. The Fort Sill–Henrietta trail, previously used, lay to the east and followed the East Cache and Cache Creek almost due south to the river.

Blocking their loads down the steep south bank of Post Oak would have been but a minor matter to these now seasoned freighters. The streambed was hard-packed sand, and the north bank was low. From there to their destination the only obstacle would have been scattered scrub oak that would have had to be cut away from time to time.

I know from experience that the freighting of this lumber bordered on a feat worthy of Paul Bunyan and his blue ox Babe. I have made the following estimates on a minimum base: 15 heavy freight wagons,

30 men, 120 oxen or 90 mules, plus a cook wagon and team and two cooks. I figure twenty days for the outward part of the trip and five days to unload and return to Wichita Falls. Seven days of this time, in my opinion, would have been used up in fording the Red River. It is entirely possible that the freighters found it necessary to unload half of each wagonload for the river crossing. This would have necessitated two trips for each wagon, besides the time consumed in unloading and reloading. Nor have I made allowance for time lost because of bad weather or waiting for streams to run down. I am quite sure the freight cost was much greater than the cost of the lumber at the Wichita Falls lumberyard.

All this is hard to imagine now. When one crosses the Red River at Burkburnett, on a modern highway bridge, and sees the wide expanse of sand, he can easily visualize the freighters' problem. But when he approaches Deep Red Run on a graded and paved highway and crosses the creek itself, he will miss the drama of the undertaking entirely. The creek's watershed has been under cultivation for over half a century, and the depth of the stream's channel is now but a fraction of what it was in those days. There is no longer any evidence of the terraced canyon sides. Timber has been cut away. Even the pecan groves are gone. From the highways I have traveled recently there is no evidence of oxbow lakes. The constant flooding of the creek's bottom has evidently filled the lakes with alluvia. But sixty-odd years ago, when I was surveying from the river crossing north, I distinctly remember having spent six hours, one day, running three miles of line. I crossed Deep Red three times in the three miles. This meant climbing up and down the steep banks and wading the waist-deep red water and mud. When I was discussing my experiences in camp that night, I had to refer to my field notes to find out how many compass settings I had made in the three miles.

Heavy dimension lumber was used in the building of Quanah Parker's house, and it was well-constructed. Part of the house was still in use eighty years later. A few years ago the army took over the area where it stood for additional missile range, and the structure had to be moved.

Apparently Quanah left the planning of the house to his cattlemen friends, specifying only that it "face the rising sun." It was, in effect, an apartment house. Each of Quanah's several wives had her separate quarters, in addition to the general living area. I have never found a statement of how many wives Quanah had at the time the house was built. He had a total of seven from the time the Comanche roll was made out in the seventies until the country was opened for settlement in 1901, at which time five were still living. Prior to the time the rolls were made, he had two Mescalero Apache wives. The name of only one of these, To-ye-yeh, has survived. The two desired to return to their own people, and Quanah consented. There is no record of children born to these Apache wives.

One interesting story connected with the house is that in the early 1890s Quanah had fourteen stars painted on the roof, including two on the summer kitchen and two on the smokehouse. It seems that during an army maneuver a brigadier general stopped at the house to ask permission to cross Quanah's property. Quanah was mystified by the many stars the general displayed. There were stars on his vehicle, on a flag the vehicle carried, and on the general's collar and shoulders. When he was informed that the stars denoted the general's command of possibly three thousand troops, Quanah decided he, too, deserved some stars, for he had commanded even more warriors than the brigadier. Hence the stars on his roof.

Quanah, who was probably born around 1852, died in this house in February, 1911. To-pay was his last surviving wife. She died in 1962, when she was more than ninety years old. She is credited with having said that Quanah's greatness was not that he was able to lead his tribe in the ways of peace, but that he was able to bring about peace and harmony in a household of several wives and numerous children.

MOTHER'S CACTUS
AND THE COMANCHE SQUAW

EVERYTHING GREW for Mother, whether it was seeds she planted in the garden or a slip she might be rooting for a house plant in our Kansas farm home, she had a window full of plants every winter.

She and Dad were as ready to go pioneering when the Comanche land was opened in Oklahoma Territory in 1902 as they had been when they came to the Kansas frontier, eighteen years before. If mother had a regret at leaving her comfortable home, it was that she couldn't take her house plants with her.

As soon as Dad's trading store building at his chosen town of Faxon, Oklahoma Territory, was completed, Mother took over the window on the dry goods side and started assembling house plants.

To me the widespread prairies seemed a paradise. Almost before I was aware, the plains became a well-kept lawn, with a multitude of spring wild flowers, rivaling Jacob's coat in their diversity of colors. I suppose prowl would best describe what I did with every free minute. It made little difference where I went—everything was new and unexplored.

One day, in my prowling, I found the most beautiful specimen of cactus I have ever seen. In Kansas, cacti grew only in greenhouses; in the new country, several varieties grew wild. This particular cactus was about three inches high and one and one-half inches in diameter.

Its sides were straight up and down, cylinder-like, and the top was flat. In color it was a rich, dark, glistening green. The gray spines grew in a scheme, or pattern, that seemed too incredibly perfect to find in a natural state. Occasionally I've seen a rose like that, so perfect you are sure it must be the work of a gifted sculptor, instead of the hit-and-miss handiwork of Mother Nature. Its spines were so regularly spaced, with the pattern repeated over and over, that you had the impression it had come from the drawing board of a fanciful draftsman.

The spines had their origin from little nodules, about the size of half of a medium-sized garden pea. The nodules covered the cylinder and top, regularly spaced. The longer spines grew in a circle, from just below the top of the nodules and almost at a right angle to them. They were perhaps five-eighths of an inch long, fine as a cambric needle, laid perfectly flat, and interlaced with like spines growing from surrounding nodules. In addition, there was a tiny circle of miniature spines growing straight out from the top of the nodules, perhaps an eighth of an inch long, and six or eight in number.

It was very early in the morning, and the reflection of the slanting sunlight on the rich green, through the gray spines, attracted my attention. With the large blade of my pocketknife I dug the cactus out carefully, leaving a sizable chunk of the red earth around the roots, and took it home to Mother. Immediately, some of Mother's friends wanted me to bring them a like plant. In a few days I went back and hunted the surrounding area carefully, but I never found another specimen.

Mother put the plant in a Number 3 tin can, fed it her particular brand of primitive fertilizer, and placed it in the sunlight of the south window she had taken over. It made a quick and unbelievable growth. Soon it was eight or nine inches tall, and about three inches through at its largest part. With its fast growth, it lost part of its symmetry. Near midway up, it bellied out till it was perhaps an inch larger than at the top and bottom. The top bulged up a bit, giving it a slightly oval appearance.

The pattern of the spines remained constant, growing out at right angles from the nodules, one set intermingling with the spines from the surrounding nodules. The spines were not menacing, like the spines of the prickly pear and many of the other cacti, unless you made direct contact, like taking hold or swinging your hand close to the plant. Should you actually take hold, the tiny spines on the top of each nodule would get you, while if you passed your hand too closely, some of the interlaced spines would be so placed that they would bite. All in all, it was a well-protected cactus, but not a menacing one.

I don't recall how many years Mother kept the cactus sitting on the little knee-high deck built even with the bottom of the window, and I remember but one casualty. One afternoon Mother was helping in the store and waiting on three Indian women. They were the multiple wives of a Comanche living in our trade territory, and were regular store customers.

Mother and Dad made no effort to learn any Comanche, and they much preferred to have me wait on the Indian trade. At the time, I was busy on the grocery side of the store, but I was keeping an eye on her efforts to wait on the three Comanche women. We kept a number of yardsticks on each counter, so that an Indian could point to what he wanted when we didn't understand him. By custom, each wife bought for herself and her children, paying for each article as she bought it. When it came Wife Number Three's turn, Mother began having trouble.

She was the youngest of the three, and would have been the homeliest even if she hadn't lost one of her eyes. Through one of the mysteries of the world of genes, her one child, a little girl about three, was a beauty by anyone's standards. The other wives of a family always had fun with the wife who was buying. They were apparently offering free advice that was neither sought nor appreciated. They bantered back and forth, but I never knew what was being said. As far as I was able to tell, the Indian women spoke a language of their own—at least they had a different vocabulary. I was soon able to follow the men when they talked, but as it was generally expressed, "No savvy squaw talk."

I was sure Number Three was trying deliberately to be difficult. Maybe she was only trying to show off for the other two wives and for some Comanche women sitting in chairs back by the stove. We never took the stove down when spring came, as there was no suitable place to store it. It took up less space in place than elsewhere. Number Three continually refused to use the yardstick Mother tried to hand her, and by motions insisted Mother lay more bolts of calico on the counter.

Finally, apparently losing her temper, the one-eyed squaw started mouthing, ran to the south end of the counter, rounded the end, and started back north toward where Mother was standing. Mother, realizing the squaw's intentions, began mimicking her mouthings, picked up her skirts slightly with either hand, as I had seen her do a thousand times when shooing chickens or helping with the livestock around the farm, charged directly toward the little Indian woman.

Mother's mouthing was just as loud and just as unintelligible as was the squaw's, and for an instant it looked as though the irrisistible force was about to collide with the immovable object. Then suddenly Number Three braked to a stop and began running backward. Mother gave her no time to turn around.

Abruptly, the trail ended for the back-peddling intruder—she reached the little window deck where Mother's flowers sat. It was as I have said, knee-high, and the cactus sat on the squaw's side. There was nothing left for the frightened Indian woman to do but sit down, and she sat with all her accumulated momentum directly upon Mother's cactus.

I never decided which arose first, the homely little squaw or her shrieks of pain. At the first shriek, the other wives ran to her rescue. A counter-top showcase hid Mother and the shrieking Indian woman. For all they knew, Mother might be murdering their companion.

When the other wives saw what had happened, they began screaming also, but theirs were screams of laughter. Close behind the wives came the other Comanche women who were sitting around the stove, and their peals of laughter added to the bedlam.

From time to time I have read stories having to do with the stoicism of the American Indians and their ability to repress emotions—remaining indifferent to either pleasure or pain. But I assure you, this repression doesn't include an already excited squaw, clad in a calico pit-sa-quina, who unexpectedly sits on a cactus. Neither did it extend to the several Comanche women present in the store when she had her mishap. The little one-eyed Indian woman's shrieks of anguish were what you would expect to hear, even from a sedate white woman, under similar circumstances. And the gales of merriment loosed by the other Comanche women present equaled what you would expect from a group of white women laughing at a companion involved in a like predicament.

Certainly, the victim's face registered a mixture of fear and pain when she regained her feet. Then there was anger, as she looked from one of her convulsed companions to another. Finally, she managed a faint grin. This ended their shopping for the day, of course, and the group gathered back by the stove and the chairs. But until their going-home time came, little spasms of giggling and bursts of subdued merriment broke out among them from time to time.

I can't for the life of me recall whether the tiny, one-eyed Number Three sat or stood the rest of the afternoon.

WHO WAS MO-CHO-ROOK?

IT WAS a hot, sunshiny Saturday in the late summer of 1902, and it was the Saturday that they were holding horse races. They were white man's races. That is to say, each horse owner had to pay an entrance fee for any horse he wished to run in any particular race. This fee money was added to the prize money the racing committee was offering on this particular race. In an Oklahoma Indian race, anyone could enter a horse, and then everyone raced for the prize money.

A very old Indian, Mo-cho-rook, who owned two fine racing stallions and always rode his own horses whenever he raced them, was standing near the finish line, in the shade of a saloon building, holding the reins of his large sorrel stallion. He was entered in a half-mile race, on the straightaway track, and from a standing start.

When the call came for all horses in the race Mo-cho-rook had entered to proceed to the starting line, the old Indian prepared to mount. He was the focal point for all eyes. Most people, white and Indian, knew he was very old, even if they did not know that the Comanche roll showed him to be seventy-seven.

He was small, possibly five feet two or three inches tall and weighing around 110 pounds. He always rode bareback. When, with his hands on the sorrel's withers, he attempted to vault onto the horse, it quickly sidestepped. Mo-cho-rook came down on his feet and did not lose his balance, but the larger Indian boys, and some of the younger Indian men, began to give him a bad time.

It was as though they had been waiting for him to make a mistake. They were telling him he was too old even to get on a horse, let alone ride one. Some of the remarks were much less polite and even ribald. The old Indian turned his angry gaze on them and spat out an invective that tended to silence them. What he said was not in my vocabulary, and I never learned what he called them.

Then he turned back to his horse, shortened up his hold on the reins, and vaulted completely over the stallion, landing lightly on his feet, and then vaulted onto the horse's back. Then he proceeded to the starting line and won himself a horse race.

I have stood near this horse's shoulders, and his withers were higher than my eyes—possibly as high as the top of my head, five feet ten and a half inches. In other words, this horse stood seventeen to eighteen hands high.

The old fellow was almost too fabulous to be believed in. As nearly as I was able to discern, he was already a Comanche legend, though he still lived. Mostly he was held in awe by the other Indians, especially by the younger ones. Maybe he was the bogeyman the elders threatened the children with. This one time was the only time I ever saw anyone try to take liberties with him. I doubt that those young Indians would have done so then but for the presence of many white people, U.S. marshals, and Indian police.

Almost any version of the story of the one-eyed man at the three-ringed circus could have been applied to me when I hit the Comanche country in the early days of March, 1902. I had had my fourteenth birthday in January. Everything was new. Everything was wonderful. I would not have changed a single thing.

Since I am Scotch, the love of the land is as much a part of me as the color of my skin or my hair. I am not trying to sound poetic when I say that the sweep of the grass-covered Comanche prairies was soul-satisfying. West Cache Creek, then the most beautiful of prairie streams, furnished the finest fishing and swimming that I have ever enjoyed, anywhere, any time.

There were wild ducks most months of the year, snipe, kildee, plover, doves, curlew, and some bobwhite for my gun. The young of a small variety of cottontail rabbits that lived in the prairie dog towns and were called prairie dog rabbits fell to my rifle. They were superior to chickens for frying, and there were few chickens in the country.

Even the great multitude of new tasks was soul-inspiring. I went ahead with the freight wagons to the little inland town later to be known as Faxon, near where the present town of Faxon, Oklahoma, is. There was the freighting of lumber for the trading store my father planned to establish, the erection of the store building, and the freighting of the merchandise. I was clerking in the store, seeing all the new faces, continually meeting new people, and learning new names.

But none of these wonders was equal to seeing, meeting, and knowing the Comanche Indians. This was especially true when I sensed that one group of the Indians was inclined to be especially friendly toward me, and they made me feel that I was, in effect, one of them. This group was made up of the older men—the warrior group. They ranged in age from the late forties upward. I remember that in my mind I classed most of them as being in their fifties. Men obviously sixty and over were very scarce.

Since apparently all primitive people are attracted by large men, it may well be that my size helped me with my Comanche friendships. In my fifteenth year I largely had my growth. I was bigger than most men, and my muscles were well developed. Within my skills, I could do a man's work, and did. I continued to grow some until I was sixteen and was actually taller than I am now. I knew only three old Comanches that were taller than I. Quanah Parker and Comanche Jack were two of them.

I was properly thrilled. Here was living history. Here were men that had ridden the war trails to the bitter end: Adobe Walls, Palo Duro Canyon, the retreat to the Big Springs Mountains, and then the surrender at Fort Sill in June, 1875.

I had nothing in common with the teenagers near my age. They didn't work, fish, or hunt, as I did. There was no common meeting ground. What I called the Carlisle group, the older young people who had been to the Pennsylvania school and were much better educated than I, by and large ignored me. I have thought since that perhaps they were a trifle jealous of the attention the old fellows gave me. There was a conscious emotional gap between these educated Indians and the old fellows.

Soon after I arrived, an old squaw man gave me some very valuable information and advice. It summed up about like this: "If a white man wants to gain the friendship and respect of the Comanche, he must stay completely apart from the Comanche women and girls." He explained it this way. Comanche women are supposed to have no communications, other than the most necessary, with menfolks other than their own, and this applied with extra force to white men. Comanche men held their women to strict account as to their conduct, and a white man could cause a Comanche woman serious trouble, unawares, should he try to be friendly. I lived up to this rule in every respect. Then, in addition, I naturally extended to all Indian women and girls every courtesy I had been taught to extend to women of my own race. This, too, could have had some bearing.

I could not help but notice Mo-cho-rook. He was a standout in every way. To start with, he was obviously the oldest of the old Indians. He was noticeably smaller than any of the other Indian men. And what was even more obvious, he had at this time only one wife. And of all the old fellows, he had by far the youngest wife and the youngest child. He was completely antisocial. I not only never gleaned a smile, but I never even drew a grunt from him, in the five plus years that I knew him.

On the top of all this, he had about the meanest look, and the cruelest eyes, I have ever seen on a human. I was later to know Geronimo, who was being held as a prisoner of war at Fort Sill. If anyone could have run Mo-cho-rook even a close second for looking mean and cruel, it would have been Geronimo.

The only time he ever came inside the store was when he needed smoking tobacco. He would have his nickel ready in his hand, would point to the Bull Durham, and when I handed him the tobacco, he would hand me the nickel. My fattest smile never brought a change in his expression. Once he had his tobacco, he would return outside. I never knew him to stay in out of even the most inclement weather.

I soon sorted out his wife. She was a young, large-limbed girl, with the true Comanche copper color. She had a baby boy, around a year old. He was old enough to be out of the cradle board, but that first summer he was not walking as yet. He was a healthy-looking little chap and, like all Indian babies, well behaved. I was later to learn that this child was the only one ever born to Mo-cho-rook by any of the numerous wives he had had. His squaw nearly always stayed in our store until they were ready to go home, and she bought all their supplies. He was one of the few Indians who never found it necessary to run an account until Grass Money time.

Sometimes Mo-cho-rook would butcher a steer and bring at least part of it into town to sell. More properly, I should say to let people buy it. The extreme selling effort he made was to pull the tarpaulin back so that you could see the meat if you walked up. He hauled the meat in the back end of a small hack, or spring wagon, and I assume he took home whatever he failed to sell and dried it.

When you showed him the cut you wanted, he waited until you showed him how much money you had; then he would cut your meat, with an apparently very sharp hunting knife that had about an eight-inch blade. He had no scale to weigh your meat, nor did he have anything to wrap it in. You carried your meat to your home in your hand, unless you had the foresight to bring something to wrap it in. He gave you good value for your money. I recall weighing his meat only once, and it ran about five cents a pound. This was about half what a white butcher would have charged you, had there been a white butcher around.

Fresh meat was hard to get. There was no ice for the first two or three years, and a butcher didn't have much leeway in warm weather. Meat had to be sold the first day. We were entirely dependent on people who would bet that they could sell a beef out before it spoiled. Generally speaking, you only got to buy fresh meat on Saturdays, when there were the most people in town.

I was making every effort to gain a working knowledge of the Comanche language, and whenever I had a friendly Indian in the store I would be writing down the names of things and acquiring useful phrases. Several months passed before I had learned enough so that I could ask some of the old fellows about Mo-cho-rook. The young men didn't care to discuss him. It could have been that they felt he was Bad Medicine.

One day I braced an old chap who was in a talking humor. We were in a comfortable spot, and we worried the subject for a couple of hours. He knew about as much English as I knew Comanche. Obviously, much of the vocabulary that I had accumulated around the store was useless in this conversation. Later I was to talk to numerous others, and ultimately an old squaw man helped me to edit, or arrange it properly, in my mind.

I asked my friend, "Oshey-him Mo-cho-rook? He no Comanche." Oshey-him may be translated as "Who is?" "What is?" or "Where is?" according to the way it is used, circumstances, etc. I think the most agonizing time came after he had told me who Mo-cho-rook was, where he came from, and many of his peculiarities when I asked him, "Oshey-him Mo-cho-rook?" placing the emphasis on Mo-cho-rook. In other words, what does Mo-cho-rook mean? Without going through the painful steps we used to arrive at it, this was his explanation. "White man say, Comanche so cruel he makes white man's blood run cold. Mo-cho-rook means, he is so cruel, he makes Comanche's blood run cold."

This, then is the story of Mo-cho-rook, after placing all the fragments together, and with the editing of the squaw man. Sometime in the middle twenties of the last century, an unusually well-planned raid was made into Old Mexico. It was made by a leader of excellent repute. His raids had always been successful, and he always picked out a select group from the volunteers. This time he selected about a hundred young but proven warriors. Each was to provide himself with two good horses, one to have a pack saddle. The end of the raid was to be the capture of a town that had never been raided from north of the river.

It was well protected on north, east, and west by unhospitable land. It was fifty miles from the nearest water, on those three sides. This rather large ranch town sat near the head of a fertile, well-watered valley. It was twenty-odd miles to the next nearest town, with only ranches lying in between.

These people were very rich in good horses and cattle. Upward of a hundred or more families lived in the town. As the plans were laid out the Comanches would move in to well-concealed hideouts in the hills below the town. The town was too large to be taken by direct attack. At siesta time, part of the warriors would make an attack on the horse herders and stampede the horses to the west out onto the desert. After the pursuit was well away from town, the herd would be headed to the north.

As many of the pursuers as possible would be ambushed, as they would be presumably strung out. But the pursuit was not to be discouraged, and they were to be led as far away from town as possible.

Once the pursuit was well away from town, the rest of the warriors were to attack the town, where the only opposition was supposed to be the old men and the boys. The available horses would have been taken by the able-bodied men of the town for the pursuit. All the old

men and big boys were to be killed. The only exception would be
if an old saddlemaker was willing to come along and work for his life.

The women and children and all the loot were to be brought to a
central spot where the booty was to be loaded on the hundred packhorses, along with the best of the women and the children. The prisoners would be tied on and the horses turned loose so as to be driven
across the desert-like land. The plan was to start as soon as possible
and drive all night, and they would be to water before the middle of
the next forenoon.

There were to be water bags, so as to give prisoners a drink, but
no warrior was to touch water until they arrived at the rendezvous
with the warriors who had the horses. There they figured they could
safely rest a day, and then it was several hard days to the river and
safety. The leader was sure that the pursuit would not be strong
enough to follow across the river.

The horses were run off, the town was captured, all desirable loot
was placed on the packhorses, and the retreat was made safely back
across the river. But one thing unforeseen and uncontemplated happened. The women had such a fear of life as Comanche slaves that
they fought the warriors to the death. The story is that they would
even take up their children and hurl them at the warriors as though
they were sticks of wood.

The women used their butcher knives, hatchets, and axes for
weapons, anything they could get their hands on, even the children.
Thoroughly enraged, the warriors not only killed all the women, young
and old, but they fired the town against the orders of their leader, who
figured this would notify the whole countryside.

While the warriors were searching and firing one of the last houses,
they heard a baby cry and found a very young baby boy, hidden up
on the top of the wall, shoved back under the roof. This was the one
living person of all of those that had been left in the town. Though
they were many days from their womenfolks, they were able to bring
this child to their women alive. He was raised as a Comanche and
became a great warrior. He was Mo-cho-rook.

I said earlier that as nearly as I could tell, he was already a legend
among the Comanches while yet he lived. I doubt that I can remember half of the stories that were told concerning him. One was that he
would have but one wife at a time, and they soon died from overwork.
Another was that his present wife was the fourth sister he had had as

a wife, the other three having died from overwork. Neither would he tolerate a slave woman to help his wife.

According to Comanche custom, if you buy a wife and if for any reason she is unsatisfactory, if she runs away, or if she dies, you may go to the wife's father and demand the purchase price back, or another wife if there is still an unmarried daughter.

Concerning Mo-cho-rook's cruelty, it was said that he never took a prisoner. He killed all, as he came to them: warriors, women, old men, children, babies; and he took no prisoners. My memory is too faulty to give the number of scalps he was supposed to still have. One thing seemed pretty authentic. He was supposed to have a full-length lariat (approximately thirty-three feet) that he had plaited from women's hair—Mexican, Indian, and white.

I was never able to learn whether plaiting was an American Indian–developed art, or if it was learned from the Spanish. Many of the old fellows plaited excellent round rawhide ropes, and also many of them were quite proud of their horsehair lariats. Mo-cho-rook was the one and only man who was supposed to have one plaited from women's hair.

His death on October 4, 1915, at the age of eighty-nine, was slightly on the prosaic side. At least he died in bed. But he saw fit to lend a dramatic touch. He had sustained a broken hip while working with his horses. They brought a doctor out from Lawton, when he refused to go to the Indian hospital. The doctor put him in a cast, but when the doctor came back in a few days, he found that the old chap had made his wife cut the cast off. She had brought him dogwood switches from the creek, and he had plaited himself a wicker cast to hold his leg and hip. He lived only a short time.

As to his age, here is all we have to go by. The Comanche roll was made up soon after the surrender in 1875. At that time he was arbitrarily given the birth year of 1826. That means that they judged him to be fifty years old. It is extremely unlikely that even then any of the warriors who were on the raid when he was kidnapped from Mexico were alive. A little arithmetic will show that they would have been at least seventy years old. That is just older than Indians became at that time, under the conditions they lived in.

Another bit of arithmetic brings some interesting conclusions. Supposing that Mo-Cho-rook's birth year is approximately correct, that means he would have been an active warrior by the year 1844. That was seventeen years before the outbreak of the Civil War, and pre-dates the Mexican War, the last months of the Republic of Texas, and the admission of Texas into the Union.

We know when the end of Comanche independence came—June, 1875. That means Mo-cho-rook was an active Comanche warrior for a period of thirty-two years. That was thirty-two years for raids along the Trinity and the Brazos. Thirty-two years of traversing Texas on expeditions into Old Mexico. Thirty-two years to drive off the Charley Goodnight cattle, and sell them to the Spanish in New Mexico.

Then don't forget that fairly authentic story that the Comanches, during the Civil War, delivered over ten thousand head of Texas cattle to the Union contractors who were furnishing beef for the Union troops.

I think I was a bit apprehensive, as I read John Graves's *Goodbye to a River*, that Graves might meet up with Mo-cho-rook's shade and his canoe trip down the Brazos might end in disaster.

NOTE: The records at Anadarko show Mo-cho-rook as Comanche Allottee Number C-2307, his birth year as 1826, and show him to have been a Mexican captive. His allotment was about one mile west and four or five north of the present town of Faxon, Oklahoma. It passed into white hands on his death. Casual inquiry brings no information on either his wife or his child. Both did survive him.

WHISKEY NIGHTS

ONLY BY A CONSIDERABLE SEARCH could anyone be found in all southwest Oklahoma Territory lower down on the social scale than the man who peddled whiskey to the Comanches. There were reasons for his low rating, even aside from the fact that the peddler was a breaker of both the United States law and the law of the territory of Oklahoma.

At the turn of the century, the Comanche warrior was only twenty-six years from his war trails. Many considered him a savage with only a superficial veneer of civilization; dangerous when sober, he was doubly feared when drinking.

Nor was it considered sporting to tempt him, as the average old Comanche's resistance was nil. The most cogent argument against selling the Comanche liquor was financial. A dollar spent by the average Comanche family man for liquor meant his family was denied its value in necessities.

The going price of a pint of cheap whiskey from the Comanche bootlegger was five dollars. This amount would supply a family of five with ample food for a week: a twenty-four-pound sack of flour, four pounds of dry salt bacon, two pounds of good coffee, eight pounds of sugar, ten pounds of good boiling beef (the Comanche seldom fried beef), seventy-five cents for dry onions and assorted vegetables, and seventy-five cents for smoking tobacco and sweets for the children.

Most Indian families lived in meager comfort if the head of the household neither drank nor gambled. Of course, Indians who were compulsive gamblers lowered their families' standard of living also. The gambler's family had a feast-or-famine existence at best.

There is this to be said for gambling money—much of it stayed in the tribe, while money spent for liquor was gone forever. It is easy to understand why decent people deplored the selling of whiskey to these wards of the government.

One recurring incident of Comanche drinking, however, became an amusing interlude to people living close to our store. It occurred in the little inland town of Faxon, Oklahoma Territory, and began immediately after the opening of Comanche land for homesteading in 1901.

The old couple involved in the incident have children, grandchildren, and great-grandchildren living. Let's call the father of the family Old Warrior. He was one of the better-to-do Indians in worldly goods. He had quite a few horses, a few beef cattle, a good hack, a nearly-new small lumber wagon, and good harness, and the family as a whole owned several stock saddles.

But when Old Warrior and his woman came to town for whiskey they never drove. They would ride double on a little, fat, gentle mare, the kind of mount the Indians termed a squaw horse—meaning a safe horse for anyone to ride. It was on such a mount the little folks learned to ride solo. Instead of a saddle, Mr. and Mrs. Old Warrior rode on a blanket, folded so both could sit on it.

Of course the mount was a dead giveaway, as they only used the little mare when they came for whiskey. Another giveaway was that they would arrive in town near dusk, long past the time they would start for home when driving. The first year or two, when not drinking, they would take a roundabout road home. But on whiskey nights, their errand accomplished, they rode straight for home, point to point across the prairie.

Ordinarily they were a friendly family, and once their other errands were attended to, they made our store their stopping place. They always tied their horses to our hitchrack, if there was room. But when on a whiskey trip, they left their friendliness at home and never came to our store. Nor did they enter any other place of business.

For some time there was a vacant store building just to the east

of our store with a recessed double doorway at the front. Old Warrior
and his woman would take possession of this setback, spread down
the blanket they rode on, sit down and pretend they didn't see anyone
passing or hear anyone who spoke to them.

Once they were seated comfortably in the setback, they would
have a ritualistic smoke. Mrs. Warrior would produce a baking-powder
can from the folds of her blanket, take out a dried and trimmed oak
leaf, hand it to her husband, then hide the can. After wetting the leaf
with his tongue, Old Warrior would rub the moisture into the leaf
with his thumb and forefingers.

During the leaf-softening and limbering process, the wife brought
out a sack of Bull Durham smoking tobacco. When Old Warrior decided the leaf was properly conditioned, he took the tobacco sack
and carefully poured the proper amount into the curved leaf. Care
was exercised not to spill a grain of the precious weed.

Rolling tobacco into a cured leaf for a smoke is an art, or at least
an accomplishment. There probably never was a white boy in all Comanche land who didn't try it at least once. When the leaf was rolled,
it was necessary to hold it in place with thumb and finger to keep it
from unrolling again.

By the time Old Warrior finished preparing the smoke, his wife,
having caused the Bull Durham sack to disappear, produced a match.
This ceremonial consumed even more time than my telling. Everything was done in slow motion. Maybe slow rhythm is a truer description. The ritual continued after the leaf cigarette was lighted; the
husband took a few puffs and handed the cigarette to his wife; the
wife had her puffs and handed it back. This exchange continued until
the cigarette was too short to hold. They made the smoke last a surprisingly long time, but they never smoked a second cigarette, regardless of how late they had to wait for their whiskey.

I saw the same ritual performed a number of times by other old
couples, and I have seen old men smoke by themselves, but I have
no recollection of ever seeing a Comanche woman smoke by herself
or with other women. We often had as many as a dozen wives sitting
in the back of the store, but none of them ever smoked.

I questioned frontier friends about the old people's smoking. They
said the plains Indians never used tobacco like the white man.
Tobacco to the older Comanches was never a solace or a dissipation;

to them tobacco was a gift from the great spirit. What I had witnessed could be considered in the nature of a prayer or communion—perhaps you could apply the word *sacrament* to it.

I made a number of plans to observe these incidents more thoroughly, but none materialized. One was to count the number of puffs each took from the cigarette, and another was to find out who furnished Old Warrior his whiskey. The trouble was that I could only watch Mr. and Mrs. Old Warrior between the chores which needed to be done around the store. Late customers had to be waited upon; the team of little Spanish driving mules had to be hitched up for our trip to the claim, when we could finally close the store; occasionally there were letters to be mailed, so they would be sure to leave on the early morning mail hack for Lawton. These necessary duties made my watching a hit-and-miss activity.

Mr. and Mrs. Old Warrior's ritual extended to the drinking of whiskey. The bottle was always kept out of sight. When Old Warrior had the bottle opened, Mrs. Warrior held up part of her blanket over one arm in front of her husband, hiding him while he had his drink. When it was Mrs. Warrior's turn, he held up his blanket to shield her.

After the bottle passed back and forth a few times, the old couple headed for home. But they never left the bottle, so I assumed they kept some for the road. Their departure would leave me with a number of things to wonder about.

I wondered if they would make it home safely, if the little mare was trained to wait in case they went to sleep and fell off. If the weather was inclement, I worried about the two elderly people catching cold. Also, I wondered what their three Carlisle-educated children, two sons and a daughter, thought of their parents' late hours.

The old people's confidence in the little chubby mare was not misplaced. They survived each trip. I imagine Old Warrior and his wife felt they had been very discreet while in town, and that none of the white people had the slightest idea they had purchased whiskey.

I once heard a story at a Comanche gathering that may explain the care Old Warrior and his wife exercised when on whiskey trips. An old fellow told of having the record books of the old Deyo Mission. They had been left with his father, Ho-var-ith-kh, for safekeeping.

After telling of the formation of the first congregation, he turned to me and said laughingly, "You knew Old Warrior? Well, once Old

Warrior got drunk and made a scene, and they "churched" him.
Brought him up for trial in the church for being drunk. The charge
and the minutes are written in the books. They didn't throw him out,
though. Old Warrior promised to do better, and they gave him another
chance."

Maybe this explains Old Warrior's actions—riding to town and back
across the prairies instead of coming and going by the road and
coming to town just at dark, knowing that the Indians and most white
people would have left town in time to get home before night set in
and the near emptiness of the unlighted street would make it easier
for the whiskey peddler to slip him the whiskey.

CA-VO-YO, GIVER OF NAMES

I NEVER KNEW but one of the old Comanches that carried the distinction of being a Name-Giver. He was Ca-vo-yo. When the Comanche roll was made out, soon after the surrender in 1876, he was given the birth year of 1840. That only meant the government clerk figured he looked to be thirty-six years old. I remember that when I finally sorted him out as an individual, I judged him to be about the age of my father, a Civil War veteran crowding seventy.

I must have seen Ca-vo-yo first in March, 1902, but then he was one of a large number of older Comanches, whom I termed, for my own convenience, the "old fellows." That meant to me that they were old enough to have been warriors who probably had fought at the battle of Adobe Walls and been present when the surrender took place at Fort Sill.

In due time most of the old fellows became individuals to me. I learned their names, where their camps were located, the number of wives each had, if any, and their dispositions toward the white man; and being a trader's son, I learned of their bill-paying reliability, in the event credit was extended to them between Grass Money payments. If a trader extended credit, he needed to know all the wives by name and keep a record of what each wife purchased, though he charged the total bill to the husband.

95

Ca-vo-yo, who was one of the first of the old chaps to become an individual to me, was such a friendly, kindly old fellow that it was hard for me to picture him riding into battle, screaming his war cry. But by the agency's record he must have been a successful and respected warrior for approximately twenty years. Had he not been a successful warrior, none would have sought him out to name their man-child and give of his medicine.

I have tried a number of times to write Ca-vo-yo's story as a giver of names, but the trouble always is that scarcely have you begun to write about the giving of a name, when you run into *Pa-haw-cut*, the Comanche name for medicine. And it is hard to tell a white audience about Comanche medicine, because the white man has nothing through which he can identify with the Comanche's feeling about it. I thought at one time of creating a straw man by combining an individual who by faith had a guardian angel with one who believed his destiny was directed by the stars and their positions, and then to this composite individual adding one who believed in luck—one who would not leave his home for the office of a morning without his good luck charm. Then I decided that the faith of even such an individual would still fall far short of a Comanche's faith in his medicine.

When a Comanche warrior was bragging, to an audience gathered around a campfire, of some mighty coup he had brought about, he was not bragging of a personal exploit—he was telling about the strength of his medicine. From the earliest war games he played as a boy, throughout his active adult life, he was constantly training himself to be ever a better warrior. It was his way of life. Also, he sought to perfect himself in the making of arms, both for war and for the hunt. Each warrior furnished his own arms. We have a written history, more or less, for the last 175 years of Comanche warfare, which shows that the Comanche possessed neither an armory nor a commissary.

Just as he had one set of arrows for war and another set of arrows he used in the killing of the buffalo, so the Comanche had horses trained for war and horses trained to carry him alongside the buffalo, so he could loose an arrow into the rib cage of his huge quarry. But it was his individual *Pa-haw-cut*, or medicine, that allowed him to count coup early and often in the battle—that caused his horse to carry him at full speed into battle and to carry him away in a strategic retreat. The same medicine allowed his horse to place him beside the stampeding buffalo without stepping into a grass-covered badger or prairie-dog hole.

It was his medicine that enabled him to crawl into a cavalry bivouac and sever the eight-foot rope that each soldier had tied to his wrist, so his horse might graze safely during the night, and without waking the sleeper or his comrades lead the horse away.

It was his medicine that caused his wives to be friendly and congenial, one with the other. It resulted in the wives' caring for his camp, looking after his surplus horses, and bearing mostly boy babies. For none of these things did he take credit personally. But he was justly proud of his medicine that had brought all these things about, and he guarded it like a jealous lover.

To sum up the attributes of a name-giver: he needed a keen ear and an extensive knowledge of the vocabulary—perhaps a sense of humor helped—and he must have a successful reputation as a warrior-hunter and a willingness to share his medicine. Custom required him to give each individual named a supply of his medicine. Warriors often refused to give a name because it meant parting with a portion of their medicine. They feared the remainder might prove inadequate. Apparently the true name-giver's supply had a similarity to the oil in the cruse and the meal in the barrel of the widow at Zarepath, while she fed the fugitive Elijah. It was replenished as used.

My reading indicates that the Comanche placed more emphasis or dependence on the name than did any of the other Plains tribes. A warrior might carry a number of names, should he live a long and successful life. In the event a boy developed into a sickly youngster, or was accident-prone, his parents were apt to seek out one reputed to have even stronger medicine than the one who gave him the first name and ask for another name. Directly after puberty when a youth went alone to fast and pray for a vision, should his vision have particular significance, he would be given a name in keeping with the vision. But no Comanche dared name himself.

After his acceptance as a warrior, should he develop outstanding characteristics in methods, strategy, or bravery, he might be given yet another name, descriptive of his accomplishments. For example, there was the Mexican captive Mo-cho-rook, about whom I tell in another chapter. Raised and trained as a Comanche warrior, he was given this name because "he so cruel, he makes Comanche blood run cold." He became a legend while yet he lived.

Little significance attached to a girl's name. Often she was given a pet name by her mother at birth and probably not given a real name for several years. Once named, she carried that name for the rest of her life, even after her marriage.

Much of my information concerning Ca-vo-yo and name-giving came from Charley Ross, who in turn had received much of his information from his father, To-wa, and his father-in-law, Mi-he-suah, whom we called Mi-so. They and Ca-vo-yo were approximately the same age, and the three had been young warriors together. Mi-so was wounded during the first charge at Adobe Walls. With a buffalo-gun slug in his abdomen he lay all day quite near the Walls without moving, knowing that should the defenders detect any movement they would finish the job. He was rescued near evening by two mounted warriors, who, riding at full speed, picked him up, laid him across the horse in front of one of the riders, and rode out of range without being hit.

Once Charley told me of a service Ca-vo-yo rendered the older Indians who knew no English. I think I remember it almost word for word, and so I will give it as a quotation. "When the white man came to live among the Comanches, here in Comanche land, he brought many things and customs the older Indians had never seen and knew nothing about. The old men went to Ca-vo-yo, and he gave them a Comanche name for each such article and custom. The words he gave them had a particular significance for the article or customs and were easily remembered."

Then Charley gave a little laugh, a sort of chuckle, and went on, "Many old Indians had never seen a completely bald man until they saw your father, so he gave him the name Ka-hait-ze Paph. *Ka-hait-ze* is 'without'; *paph* means 'hair' or 'head.'"

I carry three vivid mental images of Ca-vo-yo. One is really a composite image. He lived in a little T-shaped box house that sits on the east bank of West Cache Creek, right where Blue Beaver Creek adds itself to the larger stream. Soon the white people who lived to the east of the creek wanted another ford. They wanted a single ford to take the place of the fords across each creek, a mile upstream. So Ca-vo-yo allowed them to construct a ford just back of his house and only feet below the junction of the two creeks. To use this new ford you had to open and close two gates, as you let yourself through his horse corral.

In about a year the Rock Island Railroad came, and they wanted to build only one bridge instead of two. So, only a few feet below Ca-vo-yo's ford, they built a bridge to take their track across Cache Creek. More years passed, and now a splendid highway bridge spans the creek, just below the spot where the now discarded railroad bridge's sawed-off piling marks its once useful evistence. Ca-vo-yo's little T-shaped house also remains.

I was courting my first sweetheart when the ford went into use. Her people lived about two and a half miles east of Ca-vo-yo's house, and our town was about two and a half miles northwest of the ford. The Girl and I used his ford many times. We each had a good riding horse, and often we were horseback. Then by diligence I rated a buggy. (It didn't have a top, but we didn't mind; we were in love.) Ca-vo-yo didn't have an arbor, and if the weather was at all clement, he and his woman would be sitting on the east porch when we went by. We would smile and wave gaily to the old Indian and his woman, and they would return our smiles and our waves. With slight variations this scene was repeated many times.

One Sunday afternoon, following an afternoon church service, we were returning to her parents' home. While I held the lower gate open for the Girl to drive the buggy through, I saw Ca-vo-yo come out, open the upper gate, and lay it back. Knowing he wanted to talk, when I drew even with him I stopped the horse. Smiling his widest smile, the old fellow approached the buggy and by the means of signs and the use of one word asked, "Is she your wife (squaw)?" Apparently he and his woman were becoming curious, since they didn't understand white man's courting. Probably, to them, we were wasting a lot of time.

When you try to describe the sign language (*maw-ta-quoip* or hand talk), it sounds jerky and disconnected. Instead it had a natural grace and flow, like unhurried water making its way over a well-worn course. The old Indian extended his right fist, closed loosely, knuckles up, in front of us. Quickly extending his forefinger toward the Girl, and as quickly closing the finger back, he extended the thumb pointing to my chest. Then he said the word "squaw" as a question—literally, "She your squaw?"

I didn't look toward the Girl. I am sure she was blushing, as I know I was. I finally managed to shake my head and stammer out a "No," as I drove away. In due time the Girl and I managed to resume our conversation, but we were careful to avoid the subject broached by our ancient Indian friend.

My third image comes from an incident that happened a year or so later. As the railroad missed our town, and a new town was started by the depot, our town moved. Some moved down by the depot, but a number of businessmen in the old town, including my father, decided to move their stock and buildings to the terminal of the railroad, about four miles beyond the new town, where the town of Chattanooga, Oklahoma, now is located. This increased my courting miles considerably.

One Sunday morning I was preparing to leave early for the Girl's home, horseback. Once there I planned to borrow her brother's buggy, take the Girl to Sunday school and church in Faxon, and return home later on horseback. As I had only one horse, he had to serve as both a buggy horse and a mount. Just when I was ready to leave, I learned that because of hard rains in the Wichita Mountains the West Cache was unfordable, and I remained at home.

Around eleven o'clock the next morning, the depot agent's wife brought news to the store. The Girl had choked to death suddenly the afternoon before, presumably from diptheria. Strep throat had not been heard of in those days. Later I was to learn that she had complained of a sore throat when she arose Sunday morning, but had been up and dressed all day. About 3:00 P.M. she was lying on her stepmother's bed, visiting with her stepmother and a neighbor woman, when she suddenly choked to death, before anything could be done to relieve her.

I started Mother to dressing, hitched up a team of little Spanish driving mules to a hack, changed clothes myself, and we were on our way. The funeral had been set for two o'clock, and when we arrived at the little church, people were already gathering. I hitched the mules to the church's hitchrack, left Mother at the church, and joined the group leaving for the railroad bridge to meet the body and bring it across the swollen creek. We took the section crew's little flatcar for the body. We arrived ahead of the cortège, which was headed by a lumber wagon conveying the body, followed by the sorrowing family and near neighbors.

Other neighbors had driven directly to the bridge. Many of them I hadn't seen in months, and one after another they shook my hand and expressed their sympathy for my loss.

Ca-vo-yo's house stood within a hundred yards of the bridge, and he and his woman walked down and stood a little apart. When I went over to greet them and shake hands, Ca-vo-yo first signed their sympathy before he took my hand. Literally his signs read, "My heart is dead and in its grave."

Afterward, from time to time, as I relived that sorrowful afternoon and recalled the many words of condolence offered me, I have had the feeling that none, not even the Girl's stepmother's words, were more heartfelt.

WER-QUE-YAH, JESUS-MAN COMANCHE

WHEN I LOOK BACK at one of my old friends or acquaintances, I am unable to see him as a composite, all classified and neatly cataloged. But attached to my mental image of him is a string of happenings or episodes. Mostly, they are a part of our association together. Others have to do with happenings before I met him, and still others took place after our association ended.

They are all attached. One might think of them as beads on a string, and in my mind I run over them, much as a religious man tells his rosary. But as they are individual happenings, complete in themselves though connected, sometimes I think of the episodes as a beautiful, high-banked stream that nature set in place across the wonderful Comanche prairie. It consisted of a crescent of deep, clear pools, each connected, by a riffle flowing over clean, tannish, granite sand, to the pool below.

Yet each pool was a unit. Sometimes it extended from bank to bank. Again it would lie along one bank or the other, with a beach of clean sand extending from the water's edge to the opposite side. Each pool was teeming with fish for the fisherman. A place to bathe for those so inclined. A site for a picnic, or if needed, a wondrous baptismal font.

So I must tell Wer-que-yah's story. I have no way to classify him, no one to compare him with, white or Indian. He was as unique as a new day dawning to the east of the slightly undulating prairie he loved.

He was born into the Comanche stone-age society, probably in 1861 or '62. Their great inland empire, Comanchería, was still intact. History testifies that it had been theirs for 150 years. But that was only the length of time the white man had known the Comanche. From 1700, their ownership stretches back into the dimness of conjecture. Some anthropologists tell us the Comanche had been a separate and distinct tribe for a thousand years when the white man first met him. In any case, in 1861 Comanchería, more than six hundred miles north and south and almost as wide in places, contained thousands of horses to be captured and claimed and millions of buffalo, deer, and antelope for the Comanche's food.

But when the Civil War ended in 1865, a great horde of restless men was released by both armies. Nearly all craved land. Each wanted a home of his own, a place to grow and expand. The Comanche, other plains tribes, and the buffalo were in their road. Comanchería and the horse buffalo culture came to an end.

Sometimes Wer-que-yah would talk a little of when the Comanche world ended for him. Somewhere, out on the Comanche prairie, in what the white man had labeled the Texas Panhandle, his group was overrun by the Army. The unwounded warriors escaped, but the wounded, the aged, and the women and children were captured and taken to Fort Sill.

The Comanche Family Record Book at Anadarko, Oklahoma, indicates that Wer-que-yah would have been fourteen, and the girl he afterward married, Peet-So, six years old at the time of their capture. This would have been in the last half of 1874 or the first half of '75.

Lieutenant General P. H. Sheridan, commander of the Army in the Middle West, was determined to bring the Indian wars to an end, once and for all. He secured President Grant's consent to place the Army of the Southwest on a twelve months a year, all-out war basis. Provisions for such an effort were assembled, including grain and forage for the horses and mules, and five columns were ordered into the field.

Lieutenant Colonel J. N. Davidson was ordered west out of Fort Sill. He commanded six troops of the 10th Cavalry, three companies of the 11th Infantry, two howitzers, and eighty-five newly recruited

Indian scouts. The scouts were recruited and commanded by Captain Richard H. Pratt (the same Captain Pratt who, a few years later, was to organize the Indian school at Carlisle, Pennsylvania, and who remained its superintendent for eighteen years, trying to turn Indian youths into imitation white men).

Colonel G. P. Buell advanced from Fort Griffin. Colonel R. S. MacKenzie marched from Fort Concho. Colonel Nelson A. Miles took the field from Fort Supply. Major William Price came eastward from Fort Bascum in New Mexico. Captain Pratt and his scouts, using pack animals to carry supplies, operated at times as a sixth unit.

General Sheridan's idea was to keep the Indians on the move so continuously that their grass-fed horses wouldn't have time to graze, nor would the Indians be able to replenish their commissary from game. (In 1874 there were buffalo on the high plains, but the white hide-hunters were rapidly bringing about their extinction.) A tracing of the movements of the different Army columns as they pursued the Indians, taken from their reports, shows their trails crossing and recrossing one another, sometimes doubling back, much like lizard tracks in the sand.

There were a number of incidents in which the Army captured numbers of women and children. I have never been able to determine to my own satisfaction which group Wer-que-yah and Peet-so were in. About the only difference it would make would be in the distance they had to walk to reach Fort Sill.

Some Army reports set out the problems incurred when such captures were made. The column had to be regrouped and a force sent back with the captives, sufficient to make sure that they would not escape or be rescued by the Indians. Medical personnel and medical supplies must be part of the returning column. Food must be taken along for both soldiers and prisoners. Wagons must be detached from the main force to haul the food, forage and grain for horses and mules, and such of the prisoners as were unable to walk. This included the wounded, aged, women with newborn babies, and children too young to walk. Wer-que-yah assured us that Peet-so walked the whole distance. There were no roads, no ferries or bridges. Streams must be waded, regardless of the weather or time of year. One thing that should be noted: the Army reports mention wounded women in some instances. Many of them fought with their men in the battles.

The wounded were cared for by an army doctor, and the prisoners were fed army rations on the long walk back to Fort Sill. Once they arrived, the prisoners were placed in a guarded prison camp. They were given tents to live in and army blankets to sleep under, and were issued regular army food rations. They fared much better than the Reservation Indians, who were living on the bounty of the Indian Department. Captain Pratt, in his book, *Battlefield and Classroom*, says the Reservation Indians protested strenuously. He wrote letters to Washington, interceding for better supplies for the peaceful Indians. When the warriors were captured, or surrendered, and returned to the post, they found their women and children healthy and well fed.

Wer-que-yah became one of our first Indian customers when we opened our trading store at Old Faxen, Oklahoma Territory. We had the name Wek-wa-a for him, and that is the name under which we carried his account when Dad extended him credit to the next Grass Payment.

Perhaps "Grass Payment" needs some explanation. As soon as Quanah Parker was named chief of the Comanches by the Indian Department, Texas cattlemen began leasing graze from him at ten cents an acre. Mesquite grass and grama grass were the principal grasses. Both are members of the cane family. Tasty and flesh-building when in the growing stage, they store up sugar when matured on the stem. Stock eat and thrive on this ripe grass, and during an open winter will stay in excellent flesh. That is to say, the grasses are a twelve months' graze.

Later, the Indian Department took over the leasing of the grass and raised the price to fifty cents per acre. This lease money was distributed to the Indians on a per capita basis. It was explained to them that this payment differed from the issue of food and clothing they had received from time to time; that was pay for the grass the white man's cows were eating—or Grass Money.

This was language all Indians could understand, and the name caught on. Later, when their land was sold and the interest on their money, held in trust by the government, was distributed twice a year, it remained Grass Money as far as the older Indians were concerned. After food, beeves, and clothing were no longer issued, Grass Money and rent from their allotments were the Indians' only income.

The incident that made Wer-que-yah stand out as an individual, instead of only another Indian customer, concerned my horse. I bought this horse to replace the little Oregon mare I sold when we came to Oklahoma. I had purchased her for $9.00 from a herd of wild Oregon horses shipped to our Kansas county seat. I bought my Oklahoma horse in the winter, and he hadn't been well cared for. I turned him out on the claim and grained him each night and morning when I fed the little mules. We drove the mules, hitched to a hack, to the claim each night after we closed the store and back to town in the morning.

When the grass came lush and green in the spring, the horse lost interest in his grain and seldom came to the barn. I hadn't seen him close up for some days, when I finally decided to bring him to town. He scarcely resembled the animal I had turned out. He had shed his winter coat, and his bay hair was as shiny as though it had been oiled and polished. A roached mane was all he needed to be ready for a show ring.

And wonder of wonders, the ticks were gone along with the winter coat. There must have been something in the green grass to cause the ticks to drop. The Texas cattle tick was the bane of all livestock. Control by dipping was many years away. I don't believe there was any relief from tick infection at the time. At least, I inquired but learned of none. Cattle brought in from the north and exposed to the ticks often died quickly.

After bringing my horse to town, I found he carried a brand, which his winter coat had hidden. As brands go, it was dainty. It was small in design, and the burning surface of the branding iron was narrow. I asked a number of people, but none of them knew the brand. One day when Wer-que-yah was buying supplies, I drew the design of the brand on a paper sack and showed it to him.

Becoming quite excited, he struck himself in the chest several times with the inside of his closed fist, exclaiming, "Me. Brother. Me. Brother." I assumed he meant it was his brother's brand. When I told him I had a horse carrying the brand, he lost all interest in buying supplies.

The horse was staked about two hundred yards from the store, and we went at once. While some distance from the horse, the Indian appeared to recognize him and began smiling and talking to him. He never bothered to step around where he could see the brand. He put his right arm around the horse's nose and his left arm over its head, pulling the head down. All the time he was standing there hugging the horse's head, he was murmuring what sounded like Comanche baby talk.

After a little while, he took his right arm from around the horse's nose and broke out with a stream of excited talk. Mostly it was Comanche, but some was English when he had the words. Then he took his left arm down and added some sign language.

While this was going on, my horse stood quietly. From the moment the Indian first spoke to him, the horse had directed his attention to him, ignoring me completely. It has always been in my mind that the horse recognized the Indian about as quickly as the Indian recognized the horse.

I doubt if I understood more than 25 percent of what Wer-que-yah was telling me, and his son, Enoch, wasn't there to interpret. He hadn't seen the horse for five, maybe so six, years. I wondered if he hadn't owned an interest in the horse at one time, or perhaps owned an interest in the brand. The horse had been raced as a two- and three-year-old. Heap fast.

Then the horse ran into a wire fence. The Indian showed me a scar denoting a bad wire cut on the left shoulder, well down toward the leg. This was something else the winter coat had hidden completely, and I hadn't noticed it. Thinking the horse was ruined as a race horse, they had sold it.

The brother lived north of the Wichita Mountains—the sale had been made during reservations days, before the allotment and homesteading. Now here was the horse, well south of the mountains. I am sure my Indian friend thought it little short of a miracle.

I rode the horse to Wer-que-yah's home many times, and to his camp on the reservation when it was Grass Money time. There he would be camped with hundreds of other Indian families for the semi-annual payment. But I don't remember a time he missed petting the horse's head and giving it a bit of Comanche baby talk.

The older Comanches contended that they needed a brand on their horses only as a safeguard from white horse thieves. They claimed to know every horse they owned, whether one or a hundred, and were able to go into a herd and pick out their horses, regardless of how many there were in the herd.

Someway, somehow, this Indian knew a horse he hadn't seen

for at least five years. His brother must have put his brand on many horses. One thing I must not forget. We had figured my horse's age, by his teeth, as possibly eight or nine years old—though after seven their teeth are not too accurate a gauge.

Some five or six miles east of the town of Cache, Blue Beaver Creek liberates itself from the mountains and, flowing south, crosses the boundary between the Wild Life Refuge and the homestead-allotment area. Just there is located the Deyo Mission.

It took its name from its founder, the Reverend E. C. Deyo, a minister affiliated with the Northern Baptist Convention. A number of my old friends were charter members of the Native Baptist Church he organized there. The Reverend Deyo was a smallish man, about five feet six or seven inches tall. He wore an auburn Prince Albert beard that was always carefully trimmed. Rich colored, it was without a single gray hair.

He was one of the two missionaries I knew who learned the Comanche tongue and could converse and preach to the Comanches in their own language. He was in our store a number of times, directly after the country opened, when there would be an Indian gathering in our vicinity.

I never learned what, if any, religious influence Wer-que-yah may have experienced before the advent of Preacher Deyo, but it was quite evident that the little missionary and his church were influencing his later life.

A big event for me was making my first Grass Money payment on my own initiative, in the absence of my parents. I rode directly to the town of Cache before going to the reservation. I collected from an Indian or two I found in town, and learned from them where some of our other customers were camped.

There must have been two hundred or more Indian families in individual camps, scattered over possibly three hundred acres. The entrance to the camp-out was on the north, and a short way inside the gate sat the Red Store, the place of business of the licensed trader. He was a merchant licensed by the Indian Department. He operated on Indian ground and was permitted to do a credit business with the Indians, and he sat at the Army quartermaster's table when the payments were made. If the Indian being paid owed an account, the trader got his money first.

Wer-que-yah's camp sat a ways to the west of the trading post, in a small grove of blackjack trees. When I rode up, he was apparently pleased to see me. I was to learn that this was the general attitude of all our Indian customers—glad we were collecting so their credit would be good until another payment. Putting away what they owed until they came home and paid us was too great a problem for them to cope with. Should they remain camped there till the rest of their money was gone, they would spend the money they were saving for our account.

Before leaving the store that morning, I took a small memo book and copied the amount each Indian owed as shown by the ledger. I believe there were only fifteen accounts in this first payment. After we shook hands, I got out my little book and started to tell Wer-que-yah how much he owed.

Then his manner changed. He seemed bothered and was no longer smiling. He began telling me to wait, "his house," for *tiwa* (white man), "then I pay." On foot, he hurried toward the south, across a bit of a swag in the prairie. I could see him all the way till he entered a tent. He came out quickly. With him was the little Baptist missionary —well-trimmed Prince Albert whiskers and all.

Whenever I had met him, the missionary had had a calm, friendly, but dignified manner. But I realized as they approached now that both he and the Indian were of solemn mien. Reverend Deyo carried a small tablet and a pencil. Almost at once, he asked, "How much do you claim this man owes you?"

I took out my little memorandum book again and showed him the amount opposite Wer-que-yah's name—I believe it was slightly over $59.00—and he wrote it down at the top of his tablet. "I asked this Indian to keep his duplicate sales slips," he told me. "I want to see how their total compares."

I was busy thinking, while my customer went over to his hack and secured a woman's old purse that had long since lost both its shape and its looks. I was wondering what sort of a box the preacher and the Indian were trying to put me in. Supposing he hadn't kept all of the slips? Suppose he was honest, but had lost some? Maybe we hadn't always given him a duplicate!

The slips were rolled up endwise and tied with a strip of bed ticking. We untied them and straightened them out, and I started reading the total of each. The minister wrote them down in a column.

Soon I came to a slip with a mistake of a dollar in the Indian's favor. It was my mother's writing. The Indian had brought back a pair of girl's shoes, taken another pair that cost more, and also bought supplies —groceries and dry goods. I called the preacher's attention to the mistake, and he agreed. "Yes, it should be a dollar more." And he wrote it down that way. When he totaled the entries, the amount was exactly a dollar more than the amount I had given him.

During the auditing of the slips, both the minister and the Indian had remained grave and distant. The atmosphere wasn't friendly. Maybe they were embarrassed. I was. I was only in my fifteenth year, though I was operating in an adult sphere. My head was only a fifteen year-old head, and the same went for my experience. It was the first time anyone had seen fit to check our bookkeeping. In a way, I was feeling accused.

But when the preacher explained to Wer-que-yah, in the Comanche tongue, that our bookkeeping was honest, there was a bit of a lilt to the missionary's voice. And now the Indian was all smiles. As we arose from the ground, he exclaimed, "Wano! Wano!" a number of times and patted my back vigorously.

Then it was Reverend Deyo's turn. He extended his hand, saying, "I want to thank you for dealing with *my people* honestly. I checked your prices. I already knew you sell to the Indian and the white man at the same price. I shall tell *my people* you deal honestly. Not all merchants treat uneducated Indians fairly."

This incident may have accounted for some of our success as independent Indian traders. We, in turn, had to depend entirely upon the honesty of the Indian. He could neither be sued, nor could a judgment be levied against him.

Several years ago, two of my nephews were living with me and attending the university. One popular song you heard each time you tuned in on a radio program was "Don't Take Your Guns to Town, Son!" It was a plea of a mother to her son, just approaching young manhood, not to go to town armed, lest some gunman might see an easy way to get another notch on his gun and kill her offspring.

I told the boys I had once received much the same advice from an old Indian from whom I tried to borrow a gun while I was badly scared. It was Wer-que-yah. It happened during another Grass Money payment at the same Cache reservation. This time Wer-que-yah's camp was southeast of the Red Store, on a dry run that had a good deal of timber along both sides of its gouge.

Nearly every payment, we collectors would hear of someone being caught collecting on the reservation by a couple of deputy U.S. marshals, who had taken his money and pistol-whipped him. Until this payment, I had never been approached by a marshal. While they carried commissions, presumably they were on the trader's payroll.

I don't think I had ever been noticed before. I went to the camps of our customers only. Sometimes it would take two or three trips over a couple of days to catch everyone. When through, I hit for home. Often I was carrying considerable money and I didn't feel like visiting.

On this occasion, I was about to miss the Per-da-sop-py camp, and one of the girls—the children had all been to school—called me. I rode to the tent entrance, dismounted, and, holding my horse, waited till she brought out what she owed. As she was paying, a single marshal riding by saw the transaction and ordered me off the campgrounds.

We were about a half-mile from the gate, and he rode on ahead. I felt sure he was looking for his partner. I had visions of losing the $300 to $400 of the store's money I was carrying, and being pistol-whipped besides. I had seen men pistol-whipped by officers, and I didn't relish the prospect.

I had already collected from Wer-que-yah, knew his camp was hidden by trees, and rode directly to him. Excited, I told him my story and what I feared was going to happen to me. I knew either he or his son, Enoch, owned a good Colt .44. I asked to borrow it.

He began shaking his head. "Gun no wano! Gun heap bad!" he exclaimed over and over. "Horse heap fast!"

He jumped up, motioned for me to follow him, and started on foot down the bank of the run. Finding a place where the bank was low, he crossed over and continued down the east side. In a hundred or so yards we came to where the run left the reservation, near where it emptied into West Cache Creek.

Someone had pulled the staples holding the wire from a couple of posts, and the wire sagged almost to the ground. My friend stood on the wire and I rode across. I thanked him and hurried on my way. I wasn't by any means over my scare. I rode in the Cache Creek timber as far as I could and put my horse to a long lope—ready to start him running at the first sign of pursuit.

During the summer, a man by the name of Smith had started a

little territorial bank in Cache. His building, which was about sixteen by twenty feet, was divided about half and half by a counter, with a sort of iron wickerwork, or grill, extending above the counter. I couldn't see anyone chasing me, but for all I knew the marshals could have beaten me to town.

I never slacked speed till I reached the bank door. I had never been inside before, but I lit running. Through the door, I began clawing money out of my pockets with both hands and shoving it through the wicker. I didn't know but what the marshals might follow me inside the bank. I told the banker who I was, the reason for my haste, and that I wanted to deposit the money. He had heard something of the ways of the guards at the reservation, and he congratulated me on my escape.

Looking back, remembering the humor I was in, how badly I was scared, I feel that had this wise Indian let me have his revolver, I would have stuck it in the waistband of my pants and, cocky as a rooster, tried to ride out the reservation gate. I knew I had broken no law.

If my guess was right, and if this guard and his partner were waiting for me, I was scared enough to try to use the gun. Someone would have been shot, and it probably would have been me. The marshals were experienced officers. Always their excuse was that they had seen the collector gambling with the Indians or selling whiskey.

These subsidized marshals always operated on Indian land, it seemed; and the only recourse was in United States Court—an expensive and long-drawn-out procedure. The collector was never arrested —just relieved of his money, whipped, and ordered off the reservation. We collectors wondered why we never heard of a whiskey peddler being pistol-whipped and having his stock and money taken from him.

Whiskey peddlers never showed till dark, and I'm sure the way out I was shown was the ingress and egress of more than one bootlegger. Already, there was a worn path.

We were quite aware that a guard was necessary on the reservation while the payment was in progress and for as long as any considerable number of Indians remained camped there. Otherwise, bootleggers and gamblers would have overrun the place. Every sizable post oak tree would have had a blackjack dealer's blanket spread under it.

But there were laws governing these practices. Collecting legitimate debts was a different proposition. This restriction was an idea of the licensed trader. It would have taken the army to have stopped many of the Indians from gambling when they had money. But as long as blackjack and three-card monte were dealt by Indians, the money remained in the tribe.

The camp-out on the reservation was dear to the older Indians' hearts. It was a reminder of the wild tribal days after the late summer buffalo hunt—the feasting, visiting, storytelling, gambling, and horse racing. There was no buffalo meat; but they had learned to eat beef, and there was plenty of money to buy it. Likewise, they could indulge in other goodies they had acquired a taste for—and the whiskey peddler came with the darkness each evening.

Mostly the visitors came from faraway tribes—people who didn't have Grass Money payments. They seemed to be old fellows, warrior age. Here, there, and yonder, you would see two old fellows squatted or sitting with their backs against blackjack trees, facing each other and visiting in the sign language. You were sure they were reriding the old war trails.

There was another string to the licensed trader's fiddle. Once an Indian failed to pay his bill to an independent trader, his credit with that merchant was gone. When out of money, he had to trade with the licensed trader. These traders' prices ran a great deal higher, and most Indians wanted to keep out of their clutches.

I got over my scare once the store's money was safe in the bank, and I rode back to the reservation. My memory is that I had seen about all of the Indians owing large accounts, and I had only the odds and ends to clean up. I never saw the marshal again that afternoon. I rode in home, eighteen miles, that night, starting after dark. Perhaps I should add that most adults with sense, large merchants from Lawton and surrounding towns, and the moneylenders set up camp in the section line outside the reservation gate. There they could catch the Indians going and coming.

Some readers may read a different meaning into the word *reservation* than I have in mind in this story. I use it here in the sense of land held back, reserved from allotment and homesteading, when the area was opened for settlement in 1901. There were three of these tracts, containing two or three sections each. One was at Fort Sill, one at Anadarko, and one just southwest of Cache. There was a licensed trading store on each tract, and the land was the property of the Indians. Reservation was the name in general use for these areas. The principal agent was at Anadarko, but for a time sub-agents were maintained at both Fort Sill and Cache. One of Quanah Parker's daughters, Laura Neda, married A. C. Birdsong, an agent at Cache. The actual Comanche Reservation period ended in 1901, when the members of the tribe took individual allotments.

In 1907 I quit working at the store and went away to school. I visited my parents from time to time and often saw some of my Indian friends in town during these visits. But I never saw Wer-que-yah again until late in the fall of 1919. He farmed some of his Post Oak Creek bottomland and had grain for his beloved horses in the winter. The day I saw him, he was selling a wagonload of husked yellow corn. The Record Book shows that he died the following September. Peet-So survived him by twenty years.

Some years after his death, my mother told me of a visit he and Peet-So made to her and Dad's home. He had heard of my marriage and that we had a boy baby. He was able to make Mother understand that they wanted to see a picture of my baby.

Mother invited them in. Wer-que-yah and Peet-so sat together, and Mother said they oohed and ahed as though it had been a picture of one of their own grandsons whom they had never seen. It was shortly after the noon hour, and, learning that they hadn't eaten, Mother prepared them a meal. After they left, she was unable to find the photo. Apparently they considered it a gift. They may even have asked for it.

About ten years ago I was told yet another story. Glenn Hagar, a druggist at Chattanooga, was the teller of the tale. His father's farm was near the Wer-que-yah home. On days when they were not needed on the farm, he and his older brother often went to the Indian's home and played with his younger sons.

There were trees to climb, Post Oak Creek to wade and swim in, fish to be caught, and cool, clear spring water to drink. There were none of these things on their father's prairie farm.

Mr. Hagar's father's people lived just west of the present town of Faxon. His father's half-sister became seriously ill with typhoid fever. There were serious doubts as to whether she would recover. One morning, while the parents were waiting for the doctor to arrive, Wer-que-yah drove into their yard.

Tying his team, he came to the house and asked about the little girl. When told how seriously ill she was, he asked if he could come in and pray for her. The parents consented. The child was in a coma, and it would not disturb her. The prayer was long and, of course, in his native tongue.

I am sure there was no doubt in his mind but that God understood Comanche. When he arose, there were tears in his eyes. He assured the worried parents their daughter would live. Wiping the tears from his eyes, he went out, untied his team, and drove away toward home.

These are some episodes I tell over in my mind, recalling Werque-yah, bringing his picture before me clearly. They are the bold brush strokes. Then they, in turn, bring many tiny details to mind as I continue to think of him.

There are friendly smiles; quick, firm handclasps; an arm held high, waving me to leave the trail and ride by his home, where, smiling, he shows me his excellent field glasses. He has seen me afar off and has waited to wave. These are the fine brush strokes that fill in the background of my picture of Wer-que-yah, Jesus-Man Comanche.

THE BONE-SETTER

~~~~~~

I LEARNED of Albert Martny's accident early one summer morning, but I was unable to go to the family's camp until the next afternoon. The night before, Dad had decided to go to Lawton, Oklahoma Territory, for a load of supplies we needed for our store at Faxon.

Dad routed me out before 5:00 A.M. to get the team ready. I stabled, fed, and harnessed them, and while they finished eating, I greased the wagon. The greasing job was a must before each trip. The wagon would travel about forty-five miles before it returned home. By road it was twenty miles each way, and there was also considerable driving around to be done in Lawton, our railhead, gathering up the load of merchandise.

The team could make the trip to Lawton, with the wagon empty, in three to three and a half hours. Dad put them in a wagon yard and let them rest while he did his running around.

One trip with another, it took the rest of the forenoon for Dad to make the rounds of the jobbing houses, order what we needed for the store, and check the two freight depots. Arrival time for freight was uncertain, but we needed to order many things from jobbing houses outside of Lawton.

When he finished his errands, Dad watered and fed the team and started loading. The last thing to be loaded was a drum of kerosene.

Its place was in the rear of the wagon bed. That way, if it leaked, it wouldn't damage the other merchandise.

The trip home took about six to seven hours. If the roads were muddy, it took longer. Dad was generally gone from home about fourteen hours, but the team had at least three hours to rest in Lawton. They couldn't make these trips day in, day out. We planned at least a day's rest between trips.

This particular morning Dad was ready to leave by the time I had the team hitched up, and I went in, hoping Mother had my breakfast ready. As I ate, she asked me if I had heard anything about Albert Martny's falling from a horse, catching his foot in a stirrup, and being dragged.

The Jim Martny family, one of the more prosperous Comanche families, was one of my own family's favorites. Jim was larger than most Comanches; many folks called him Big Jim. He was a multiple-wife Indian, and his favorite wife was the mother of two boys—Albert, then in his fourteenth year, and Earny, who was twelve. Jim's other wives' children were girls.

Indirectly, the way Mother learned about Albert's accident was that ours was one of the luckier towns—we had a doctor. Dr. McLain, just out of medical school, settled in our town with his young wife only a few days before we arrived. He built a combination office and residence across the street, and a bit east, from where Dad built our store building.

Mrs. McLain was expecting a baby before long; and when the doctor made an out-of-town call, Mother or Mrs. Cudyback, the wife of a saloonkeeper living directly across the street from the store, would sit with her. Occasionally Mrs. McLain would go to the Cudyback home or sit in our store until the doctor returned. The night before, both Mother and Mrs. Cudyback had visited with Mrs. McLain, and Mother was full of the story about Albert's accident. Mr. Cudyback picked up a good deal of gossip at the saloon he and his brother Will ran, and Mrs. McLain told what she learned from her doctor husband.

Jim Martny owned two well-bred racing stallions, and his other horses were of superior quality compared to the horses owned by most of his Comanche neighbors. I don't know how long Albert had been riding his father's horses in races, but early in 1902, when our town began holding races each first and third Saturday, Albert was his father's rider. Comanche-fashion, the boy rode bareback to save the horse the additional weight of a saddle. He rode in his sock feet, as this helped him to grasp the barrel of the horse better. Many races were run from a standing start.

Comanches, who learned about horses from the Mexicans and Spanish, mount a horse from the right. (All horsemen of Europe except the Spanish mount from the left, and we Americans copy them.) This time Albert was using a stock saddle to exercise the larger stallion. The half-wild animal bolted as Albert started to mount. Albert fell, and his right foot caught in the stirrup.

The frantic horse dragged the boy, dangling from the stirrup, through the timber and underbrush of West Cache Creek bottoms for more than two hours before the father could rope it. They sent for the white doctor right away; but when Dr. McLain saw the boy's condition, he felt death was only a matter of hours, and the setting of the bones and cleaning of his wounds would only subject the boy to additional pain.

He left them a supply of morphine tablets to give the injured boy, should he regain consciousness before dying. This was quite in keeping with the practice of medicine at the turn of the century. Doctors passed out morphine tablets as though they were a new cough drop they were advertising. No other medicine, other than quinine, was in as great supply or as cheap. Most families had at least an eight-ounce bottle of laudanum on the pantry shelf. In addition to its value as a medicine for humans, amateur horse-doctors found it useful.

When Jim's wives learned through Earny that the doctor held out no hopes for Albert, they went into the death wail, even before the doctor could leave the camp.

The foregoing is practically all the community ever learned directly about Albert's accident and the events immediately following Dr. McLain's departure. The rest of the story must be told much as a prosecuting attorney presents circumstantial evidence to convict a defendant of a crime when there are no eyewitnesses.

With Dad away I couldn't leave Mother alone with the store, and the day following an arrival of a load of freight was always a busy one. Besides the team to be cared for and the trade to be waited on, there was merchandise to unpack, mark, and put on the shelves. On nearly every load there was a fifty-five-gallon drum of kerosene to be pumped into the store's container.

It was the middle of the afternoon before I could saddle my horse and leave for the Martny camp. Jim's family allotments, about six miles down Cache Creek, were the last individual Indian land. When the creek left his land it entered the Big Pasture Reserve, the ranch country. His allotments adjoined the reserve on both their south and east sides. There were two roads into Jim's camp, and both dead-ended. One, the road I used to reach the camp, came from the west and north; the other ran north from the camp to a gate into the reserve. The latter road was the one Jim used when going directly to Lawton or to the subagency at Fort Sill. A concept of the camp's isolation will help the reader to have a clearer understanding of sub-sequent events. As I have said, the evidence is mostly circumstantial.

I found Albert conscious, lying on his platform bed under the family's large brush arbor. As I remember it, their arbor was the largest family arbor I saw during the time I was in the Comanche country, probably thirty by thirty-six feet. It had a clearance of a full six feet at the edge or eaves and probably eight feet at the center. It was large enough for platform beds for all, besides a sizable living space. I saw larger arbors constructed for camp meetings, but not for family use.

Albert's mother left us boys to our talk, and I took over the job of switching the flies away with a leafy twig. Of course Albert knew nothing of the happenings, after the first few jumps made by the excited horse, until he regained consciousness, completely trussed up in splints. Beyond question, he was the worst broken-up human, to be living, I ever saw.

His right arm and leg, splinted, were lying in troughs made from pieces of wood from goods boxes. At that time all canned goods and food sold in cartons, like oatmeal and crackers, were shipped in wooden boxes. I imagine the Martny wives had saved the pieces to start the campfire.

The breaks in this arm and leg were compound fractures. That is to say, one or both bones from each break protruded from the flesh. The breaks in the left arm and leg, which were simple fractures, were held in place with splints from the same material, but were not in troughs. The splints were wrapped and padded with faded calico rags.

Here and there on the limbs and along the side of the body pieces of flesh were gouged out where the horse had stepped on the flesh. His racing shoes must have been new, for they made clean cuts.

Albert's scalp was torn loose from just above the hairline on his neck to about the crown of his head. This had been stitched back in place with stitches about three quarters of an inch apart. Along the stitches, and on all the wounds that were uncovered, a white powder had been sprinkled. I assumed that this was powdered calomel, as it was supposed to be the best repellent for screwworm flies.

Albert's body was exposed to the warm, dry air, aside from his breech-cloth or G-string. This is traditional covering for a Comanche boy's private parts, front and back, from the time he reaches puberty and throughout his life.

From this point, aside from a meager statement made by Big Jim, we are wholly dependent on circumstances for our reconstruction of what happened. Albert, Earny, and neighboring Indians contributed nothing to the overall information. Of course, no one wasted time trying to learn anything from the women. But the circumstances confront us with a succession of phenomena, or miracles, whichever you choose to call them.

The white doctor was barely gone when an itinerant cowboy rode into camp and asked for food. Hearing the women wailing, he learned of Albert's accident and offered to set the broken bones. He washed and cleansed the wounds and protruding bones with yellow laundry soap such as the women used when they washed clothes in West Cache Creek. (I can testify about the soap. We sold many, many cases of it over a period of years. Its trade name was Lenox, but I don't remember who manufactured it. It was carried by all jobbers and was the cheapest laundry soap on the market. We sold it at a nickel a bar, six bars for a quarter.)

Should Big Jim's soap story sound far-fetched, let me introduce some corroborating testimony. Jim Carter, who for many years was both a member of the Oklahoma City police force and my personal friend, told me this story. When he was around nineteen, he was a line rider for a ranch out from Olton, Texas, in the Panhandle. Along with a lad two or three years older, he lived in a line shack about fifteen miles from ranch headquarters.

One noonday, after they had eaten, Jim started to mount his horse for his afternoon chore. The horse started bucking before Jim was in the saddle. Somehow his weight came down on his left leg extended across the saddle seat, and the bone in the upper leg snapped, about halfway between the knee and the hip. Of course, Jim fell to the ground. One end of the bone, thrust through the flesh, gouged into the dirt.

His partner carried Jim into the line shack, broke out a bottle of whiskey to calm him down, and proceeded to set the bone. First he washed the protruding bone in soapsuds made from a bar of yellow laundry soap—the only soap or disinfectant they had. Then, slipping one boot off, the amateur bone-setter put his heel in Jim's crotch and pulled the bone back in place. He tore up a cotton blanket into strips, wound strips of the blanket around pieces of wood from a goods box, put one splint under the leg and one on the opposite side from the wound caused by the bone, and bound them in place with other strips of the blanket.

As nearly as Jim remembers, the wound stopped bleeding and was not bandaged. But Jim wasn't too sure from here on; he was paying closer attention to the whiskey bottle.

His companion put the rest of the whiskey and a bucket of water by the head of Jim's bunk and set out for the ranch. The rancher sent a cowboy for the doctor, and they laid a mattress in a lumber wagon and started for the line shack. There Jim was lifted onto the mattress, and the long, slow, rough trip to the ranch began. The doctor met them on the way. It was night, but he examined the leg by the light of a kerosene lantern. Aside from adding more splints and telling them not to stint on the whiskey, he okayed the job, and the trip to the ranch was resumed.

The doc told them he didn't know anything that was better to clean a wound than laundry soap. Jim was left with a slight impediment in his walk, as if the one leg was a bit shorter than the other. It was a good enough leg for him to serve long years on the police force, in various capacities. He was finally retired because of advanced age.

Time must have been an element in saving Albert. Here was a tramp cowboy faced with a job which would tax the resources of the receiving room of an outstanding modern hospital. He had to complete his job before dark, as the only available light would have been a kerosene lantern with a number one wick. Whatever help he could receive would come from Jim and Earny. All instructions to Jim must be relayed through Earny. The instructions must be reduced to language Earny could understand before he could relay them to Jim. Earny was a good interpreter, an unusually bright boy for his age; but after all, a twelve-year-old Indian boy has only a twelve-year-old Indian boy's head.

My personal feeling is—and I believe anyone who lived around the plains Indians at the turn of the century will agree—that the greatest miracle performed that afternoon was calling the Martny wives back from the hypnotic state of the death wail. This is a deliberate, self-induced mental condition; and when the women have been in it for a sufficient time, they become impervious to pain. They slash their breasts, bodies, and legs; and if the state continues long enough —say into the third day—it is climaxed by their whittling off a finger with their butcher knife. Generally it is the forefinger of the left hand. Women in this thralldom seem to have a high coagulatory content in their blood. Evidence of women's bleeding to death from self-inflicted wounds, when in this hypnotic state, is nil.

Possibly this blood property is a result of the women's heavy meat diet, or it may be a chemical change in the blood brought on by the severe hysterical state under which they are laboring. One thing old plainsmen are agreed on: Indian women are extremely dangerous when in the wail, and even their own menfolks give them a wide berth.

Because this state is deliberate and self-imposed, they resent being called back to normalcy. It is entered into to escape a sorrow—something they cannot face in their normal state. Perhaps their minds become as blank to sorrow as their bodies do to pain. In a way it is the kind of thinking a drinker uses, when he stultifies his senses with liquor to forget his inadequacy. Of this I am sure—I could never myself have the courage to call three wailing Comanche women back to sanity.

I think of three things happening that day that we can properly label phenomena. First is the dragging of this boy by a frantic horse, through the brush and timber of West Cache, for more than two hours, without the horse's ever once kicking or stepping directly on Albert's head or rib cage. The Bone-setter must have diagnosed these facts, and Dr. McLain must have overlooked them.

Phenomenon number two is a strange cowboy's riding through the country, chancing upon this isolated camp, and seeking food at that exact time. Number three is, of course, that this particular stray cowboy had the courage and willingness to take on a job shunned by a trained, educated doctor, and the skill to turn out a workmanlike job.

Let us review what we know concerning the Bone-setter. Dr. Mc-Lain insisted that the cowboy's work indicated he possessed surgical training. His stitches were put in with a surgical needle and catgut suture, and he had a limited supply of powdered calomel. Excepting for the powdered calomel, these things were unlikely appurtenances to be carried by an itinerant cowboy. With the circulation of these facts, the tongues of the curious wagged.

The only other testimony comes from Jim Martny, Earny interpreting. No one else acknowledged knowing the cowboy or having seen him. Nearby ranch-owners and their ranch hands would not admit to knowing any cowboy who could fill the bill. They knew of cowboys who had set a bone or two; but this was a multi-fracture, a wholesale affair, along with the job of cleaning and stitching Albert's scalp back in place, besides caring for the numerous horseshoe wounds.

Approximately in these words, with Earny translating, Jim told of the cowboy, and he never varied from it: "Cowboy come to camp just after white medicine man leave. Him say he hungry. We feed cowboy. Him say he cowboy medicine man. Him set Albert's bones. Cowboy ride away north.

"Him look like all cowboys look. All cowboys look alike. All have mustache. All have big hat, high-heeled cowboy boots. All wear jeans pants and calico shirt. All have big gun in belt. All have good saddle.

"Horse him different. I tell about horse. Him sorrel so high," and Jim pointed to his chin.

"Horse come long way. Horse tired. Cowboy tired. Horse have white face. One white foot." And Jim made the necessary motions to help Earny finish the description of the horse: blaze face, left front foot white.

There was never one word as to how the long afternoon progressed, other than the use of the yellow soap. This was one of the few specific questions Jim seemed to understand. Like most Indians of his day, he found "No savvy" a convenient way to dodge any question he didn't care to answer.

Never a word as to how the women behaved. No word as to when Albert regained consciousness—whether it was during the ordeal of having his bones set or afterward. He was conscious when Dr. McLain drove his buckboard out, the afternoon of the second day, to dress the wounds. This seems to have been an instruction from the cowboy, to have the white doctor come out the second day.

Dr. McLain added little to the meager supply of facts. I believe he went out only two times. The wounds were all completely scabbed over, with so sign of infection, and he told the Indians he wouldn't be needed. He left them a supply of powdered calomel, with instructions to use it freely to repel screwworm flies. This was something the Indians savvied, guarding against the screwworm fly. It had been their enemy for countless generations.

We mustn't neglect to give Albert's healthy body, and his ancestors, credit for his ready healing, the quick, strong knitting of his bones—plus the stoicism with which he lay there through the long hot summer, letting nature take her course. (I took occasion, once, to congratulate a surgeon on the job he had done on my son's broken wrist. He replied that much of a surgeon's success depended on the patient. "Your son got a good wrist and arm because when I told him not to use it, he obeyed. Then when I told him to use it, though it hurt, he used it.")

Albert remained out of school when fall came, and about Thanksgiving time he made his first trip to town horseback. I had been working out in the tent wareroom. Finishing my task, I returned to the storeroom and found Mother talking to Albert. Jim was standing there, face abeam, as Mother told Albert how well he looked.

His hair was long enough to cover the scalp scars, and his clothes covered the other marks of his accident. There was not a scar on face or hands. He was using all four of his limbs. His right leg was shorter, apparently, than the left, but for some time he limped on both legs.

By this time, much of the resentment over Jim's story had subsided. Most people took the story at Jim's value. Besides, they had things of greater interest with which to occupy themselves. But the overcurious, and those who had a "thing" about Indians in general, tried to create a feeling against the Indian family and against the cowboy Bone-setter who had saved the unfortunate boy's life.

Some people who didn't draw claims, and some who did, resented the Comanches' having all the good bottomland along West Cache, the water, and the timber. I think it would have helped if the government had called the land the Indians kept reserved land, instead of allotments. This would have accented the fact that all the land had belonged to the Indians and that they had sold only such land to the government as they, the Indians, didn't wish to keep. The faultfinders professed to feel it was all government land, of which the Indians were given the first pick.

The meager description of the Bone-setter, compared to the detailed description of the horse he was riding, fed the flames of those who resented Indians and everything concerning them. They promptly accused Jim of laying a false scent. In number, sorrel horses are in the minority compared to other colors. The dissenters contended that while officers were hunting for a fugitive mounted on a tired sorrel horse, the hunted, on a fresh horse of a different color furnished by Jim, would escape.

Of course, there never was anything to indicate positively that the Bone-setter was a fugitive, nor did any representative of the law ever appear, hunting a mysterious cowboy. The fugitive idea was a product of minds wishing to believe the worst of anyone who gratuitously aided an Indian.

Some insisted that the mysterious Bone-setter hadn't left, but was being harbored by Jim. They wished to form a posse and make a search along West Cache Creek, on Jim's allotments, for the secretive cowboy's camp.

The wildest theory brought forward was the idea of the good Samaritan's having been done away with by one of Jim's squaws. This presumed that Albert regained partial consciousness about the time the Bone-setter finished his job and cried out in a delirium of pain. A nearby squaw used her butcher knife, the theory went, before Jim could rescue their benefactor.

To some, this explained the disappearance of the Bone-setter and the exactness of the description of the sorrel horse. The body could be disposed of in either of two ways. Stripped of its clothing, it could be weighted down in one of the deep holes along Cache Creek. There the garfish would soon dispose of the flesh, while an unbranded horse turned into Jim's herd would go unnoticed. Another suggestion had Jim stripping the body, tying it on a horse, and making a night trip into the Pasture Reserve. There the body could be left for the coyotes and buzzards to dispose of. (When the Pasture Reserve was opened in 1906 with a family on practically every quarter-section, a number of skeletons were found, one only about four miles from Chattanooga. A man named Richardson found it on his homestead. The writer went out the next morning, with the sheriff and county attorney, and helped gather up the bones.)

But even the cruelest gossip, if rehashed long enough, becomes tiresome, and in due time the vicious-minded turned their talents elsewhere. During the five years I remained in the community, nothing was added to, or subtracted from, the mystery of the Bone-setter.

By the time the town started holding races the following summer, Albert was recovered sufficiently to ride his father's horses, and he returned to the Indian boarding school in the fall. When he and Earny returned home at Christmas, Jim brought the two boys to the store to exhibit them in their blue school clothes. Albert had grown, unbelievably. Jim and I put him between us, and he was almost as tall as we were. Earny was rejoicing at his brother's growth. It meant he would now ride his father's horses in the races. The school people allowed Albert to wear his hair long enough to cover his scalp and neck scars, and he was truly a fine-looking young Indian man.

The Comanches had a word for him, but I was not to learn it for some time. The word is *Tao-yo-vis-ses*, meaning a fine-looking young man of warrior age. The story is that in camp, after the fall hunt and before the bands went their separate ways to winter quarters, the boys who had become young men would clean and polish their finest horses. Then, with their womenfolks assisting, they would carefully comb and braid their hair, rub oil into their skin until it glistened, don their gaudiest breechclout and moccasins, and ride bareback slowly through the camp, single file.

The camp might well be strung for some miles up and down a creek or stream. The boys were joined by the girls who had reached puberty but were not married. The girls, hair in two long braids, painted and dressed in new buckskin dresses and leggings, were equally proud of their bodies and bearing. The girl's name corresponding to *Tao-yo-vis-ses* is *Nai-vi-se*.

The older Comanches considered this the finest sight in all the world. Everyone came out of the tipis, young and old, warriors and chiefs, and they cried out over and over, "Tao-yo-vis-ses! Nai-vi-se!" There before them was the tribe's future—its chiefs, its war leaders, its warriors, and the bearers of the tribe's men babies. Here were "The People" of tomorrow's tomorrow.

Now Albert Martny, who but for the skill of the unnamed Bone-setter would surely have died, was a handsome young warrior. You may be sure, come the summer Grass-Money time, Albert's womenfolks presented their *Tao-yo-vis-ses* with pride.